I pray y⸗

happy Marriage

17/09/17

MAKING YOUR
MARRIAGE
WORK

Maama's Practical Wisdom
for a Lasting, Happy Marriage

EYITAYO DADA

JEREMIAH HOUSE
PUBLISHING

Toronto, Ontario

Cover design by Joshua Crandell
Published in Toronto, Ontario, Canada by Jeremiah House Publishing.

Unless otherwise noted all Scripture quotations are from the New King James Version. Copyright 1982 by Thomas Nelson, Inc. Used by permission. All rights reserved.

Scriptures marked NASB are taken from the New American Standard Bible, copyright 1960, 1962, 1963, 1968, 1971, 1972, 1973, 1975, 1977 by the Lockman Foundation. Used by permission.

Any italicization or words in brackets added to scripture quotations are the author's addition for emphasis or clarity.

Dada, Eyitayo, 1962-, author
        Making your marriage work : Maama's practical wisdom for a lasting, happy marriage / Eyitayo Dada.
Includes bibliographical references.

ISBN 978-0-9940534-4-2 (pbk.)
ISBN 978-0-9940534-5-9 (epub)

Family & Relationships: Marriage & Long-Term Relationships
Religion : Christian Life - Love & Marriage
Interpersonal Relations

Special Market Sales
Organizations, churches, pastors and small group leaders can receive special discounts when purchasing this book and other Jeremiah House Publishing resources. For information, please email info@jeremiahhousepublishing.com

Printed In Canada

I would like to dedicate this book to God my Father, my Lord Jesus Christ, and the Holy Spirit.

I would also like to dedicate it to the love of my life, Amos Dele Dada. The man I call "Mine".
My husband, best friend, pastor, mentor and teacher.

Though it's been thirty-seven years since I met you and over thirty years since we said "I do", it seems just like yesterday we decided to do life together and I am forever grateful.

Thank you for making our marriage work and making my dream of having a lasting, happy marriage a reality.

CONTENTS

ACKNOWLEDGEMENTS

Thank you to:

My family for putting up with me during this intense writing process.

My husband, Amos Dele Dada
My five daughters and two sons-in-law,
Ade and Dara, Joshua and Toyin, Ife, Tobi and Debbie
My two granddaughters (and the many more to come),
Josephine and Marantha

Jeremiah House Publishing
Especially, Toyin and Joshua Crandell
For your help getting this book from an idea and my many speaking engagements on this topic to a beautifully crafted, published book.

Amos Dada, Tobi Dada, Dammy Oyebode and
Taryn Lee Dube for your assistance in proofreading.
Wale Ajayi for collating and typing the original material.

I believe that many marriages will last longer and be much happier because of your efforts.

God bless you.

Foreword

Apostle James (James 3: 13-18) describes what worldly and Godly wisdom look like, and reading this book you'll see a clear practical demonstration of what pure Godly wisdom looks like when mixed with life experiences by a Godly person.

I have known Evangelist Eyitayo Dada (her husband, Pastor Dr. Amos Dada and family) for about a decade, and I've been blessed to visit them in their local assembly. I have seen their consistency of faith and demonstration of what they teach and how they have sown in the lives of children of God, to bring glory to our heavenly Father.

In this amazingly simple book to read, Maama (as she is fondly called) has brought Godly wisdom from the written word, the leading of the Holy Spirit and her life experiences, which includes thirty years of marriage, being a parent, a pastor's wife (taking care of people's needs) and a working professional, to help young and older couples alike navigate their marriage seasons.

I have been blessed to write twelve books and to speak on marriage in over forty countries - so I know a thing or two and I highly recommend "Making Your Marriage Work" to you.

I pray that as you read, Holy Spirit will bring revelation that will transform your marriage and home for His glory.

—Bro. W. Femi Awodele
Executive Director
Christian Couples Fellowship International Inc.
Omaha, NE, USA

Preface

This book has been created to help marriages that are either thriving or struggling learn wisdom keys that will help you to have a lasting, happy marriage. In light of this, the book has been divided into two parts. The first is a reminder of the very basics of what marriage should look like, its purpose and original intent as well as some specific wisdom for the husband, wife and insight on what to do when you have children in the mix.

Part Two is the Marriage Manual. It is centered around dealing with and even thriving in the midst of the conflicts that many marriages face. I have chosen to discuss the most common challenges I have witnessed in my years of marriage counselling. After which I address some foundational principles to keep joy in your marriage and avoid divorce.

I advise you to take time to read this book through once with your spouse, and then to keep it as a go-to when you are addressing different challenges that life throws at your marriage.

Get a copy of the book and give it as a lifeline to couples who are at their wits' end and don't know where to go to improve their marriage. Give a copy to a newly married couple so that they build on the right foundation and do not make the same mistakes that so many people have made, which has put their marriages on life support.

This is also a manual and resource for marriage counsellors, Pastors and parents (biological and spiritual) with advice for how you can help married couples who are desperately trying to save their marriage but don't know how.

I know you will enjoy it.

—Maama

Part One

Building A Foundation For Happiness In Marriage

1

Let's Sit And Talk

A good marriage isn't something you find;
it's something you make.
—Gary L. Thomas

Hello there Mr. and Mrs., my name is Eyitayo Dada and everyone calls me, Maama. I would like to talk to you about how you can have a lasting and happy marriage. I have counselled many husbands and wives just like yourself.

Some have been facing challenges that seemed hopeless while others have been in a continued honeymoon status and choose to come to me to learn how they can maintain the joy and friendship in their marriage.

Too many married couples are at a point where they

wake up in the morning and can't even recognize the person they're in the bed with. "Is this the man I married?" "Is this the woman I professed to love with all my heart?" For these people, it may feel like they are married to an old-time friend who has become a stranger.

Whatever part of the spectrum your marriage currently falls in, there is something here for you.

There are many books on marriage and many people who give counsel and advice to couples. I learn from and appreciate a great number of them. Where I come into the conversation is taking all that biblical knowledge you have heard over and over again and making it practical and applicable to your modern day marriage.

But First Something About Me

I am an African Canadian wife and mother of five daughters. Two of them are currently married, one is recently graduated, the other is in graduate school and the third is, at this time, just getting started with University. I'm delighted to say that for our two married daughters, this same advice (and my advice on choosing the right partners) has led to them finding young men with whom they share a passion for Jesus, live with a common vision for the future, and their marriages are a source of joy to them.

But let me take you into a bit of my history. When I was growing up, I was surrounded by a lot of miserable marriages, and I saw many people who had become bitter and unhappy because of the marriages they were in. But it wasn't just the fact that they were in a state of constant unhappiness that made me passionate about seeing marriages succeed, what marked me in those early years was the level of hypocrisy I witnessed. Married couples lived like arch-enemies at worse, and co-tenants at best. Yet while in that state, they would put on this "happily married" couple facade to the outside world.

In my early years, the deception was remarkable. It seemed they were so good at portraying this perfect marriage facade that their private despair was completely hidden from others but not from themselves. It was commonplace to see people from outside, who did not know what was really happening inside the home, desperately want to have their marriages resemble these hypocritical shows. If only they knew what they were wishing and praying for.

Because of that experience, as a child I prayed from the bottom of my heart that I would be truly happy when it was time for me to be married. Not just at the beginning but throughout. At one point I even told God that if

> *There is no more lovely, friendly and charming relationship, communion or company than a good marriage.*
> *—Martin Luther*

my marriage was going to be anything like what I was seeing in the people around me I would rather stay single.

I can't explain to you just how much I wanted not just to be married but to be happy in my marriage and have a lasting one. And God heard my prayer. Many years later, a man called Amos Dele Dada came into my life and my dream became a reality.

Over our years of marriage, we have been through many different seasons and there has been a level of happiness, peace and joy that has remained constant even in the most trying times. Though both of us have changed much over the years and walked through some of the issues I will be discussing, we have come to know each other more intimately because of them, instead of becoming strangers.

In my years of ministry, I have continued to come across young and old who are absolutely miserable in their marriages. Instead of enjoying their marriages they are enduring them and that breaks my heart because I know it does not have to be so.

Now, if you have heard advice that you can expect to be happy in your marriage for the first few years during the "honeymoon" stage, but that afterward "reality" sets in, this is the part of the book where I'm asking you to throw that advice into the garbage! Quick, quick!

I remember when I was getting married, a lot of people said to me "Ohhh, you and your fiancé are so happy. I give you five years. After five years, the honeymoon is over." I used to tell them, "God forbid! Every year of my marriage will be a honeymoon."

And over thirty years later, I can confidently and happily say that it has been the case. The reality is, no matter what happens, you can enjoy your marriage.

Seeing the sharp contradiction between the marriages I witnessed as a child, the marriages I see around me and what I am currently living in, I could not take for granted the keys of wisdom that have helped myself and my husband all these years. Not just in preserving our marriage but in maintaining the joy, excitement and friendship that brought us together over thirty years ago.

Because of those experiences, I also cannot pretend that

most marriages look and feel like ours. So I have made it my life's mission to share these wisdom keys for a lasting, happy marriage with as many people as possible.

My husband became a pastor soon after we got married, though becoming a pastor's wife was certainly not part of my original plan (that's a story for another day). My experience as "Maama", counselling many men and women through their marriages and seeing these wisdom keys turn their marriages around has inspired, or rather, demanded that I convert what I teach into a format that many more people will have access to.

Unity - The Way To Overcome

Over the past thirty years, I have spoken to young and old couples, financially established, those who are struggling and the spectrum in between. I have met with people from different cultures - intercultural or interracial couples and counseled couples that are dealing with terminal diseases or other illnesses, infertility, job loss, no income, debt and many other difficulties that come up in the course of marriage. In all of my experience, I have found that people in bad or broken marriage relationships are the most miserable of all.

I have also seen that when a couple is bound together in the true meaning of love, unity and submission that God ordained, they can overcome any and every external adversity of life together. However when they have built a wall between themselves, it becomes a bitter environment.

I say this often, "You can have no money, no children, and nothing else but if you are in a good marriage, you will be happy. Yet you can have everything that others are praying and crying for, and if you are in a 'bad' marriage, you are miserable." If that is you, there is hope. Your marriage is not stuck in this unbearable place.

I firmly believe that each of us can actually, really, have a happy marriage not just for a year or two, but forever.

While you read, do not bother yourself with what your spouse is supposed to do to help make your marriage better. Instead, focus on what you can do. Women, while you read the chapter for husbands, apply those lessons to yourself and likewise men.

> *The reality is, no matter what happens, you can enjoy your marriage!*

At the end of the day, your marriage is what you choose to make it. Not what "she" or "he" made of it.

I know for a fact that God can, and does turn hopeless looking situations around. This includes "hopeless" looking marriages. But like everything else, you will have to cooperate with Him. You have to be willing to change your thinking and behavior as you read this book otherwise the wisdom keys hidden here will not help you.

Make the choice today that your marriage will work. That you will not endure your marriage but enjoy it!

Before you return to your old habits of blame, accusation or raising up past wrongs, STOP - look at the situation objectively and ask what can I do differently to make this marriage work?

Remember, you can't change who you married but you can make changes in yourself that - over time - will give birth to a new marriage.

Here's to your lasting joy!

2

The Plan Of God For Marriage

We will never obtain God's kind of marriage simply by going along with the crowd, doing what everybody else does. We have to dig deep into the heart of God to discover His principles.

—MYLES MUNROE

Before we get into the challenges and conflicts that many face in marriage, we have to begin with its definition and purpose. If you want your marriage to be and stay healthy, go back to its foundation.

What Exactly Is Marriage?

Marriage is your expression of love and a sign of commitment to each other. It is designed to mirror our

Creator's unconditional love for us. It's a love that you choose to give always. It is not about you coming to receive, but choosing to give. It provides an opportunity to grow in selflessness as you serve your spouse and children. Your marriage was the inception of a new family, a new genealogical line—and is a lifelong commitment. When you can both love each other with that unconditional love, contentment follows and joy abounds.

Marriage is a formal union, a social, and legal covenant between two individuals (male and female) that unites their lives spiritually, legally, economically, physically and emotionally. It is a covenant unbreakable by wavering emotions, difficult circumstances or unforeseen situations. This union mirrors the one between God and His church.

Marriage Is Ordained By God
It Was His Idea

The first marriage was in the Garden of Eden between Adam and Eve. Take note that even when Eve offered Adam of the fruit from the tree of the knowledge of good and evil, God's solution was not to break up the marriage covenant that He had placed them in.

Not even after Adam blamed Eve for his disobedience by saying "the woman you gave to me, gave me this fruit," did God make it a justification for their separation.

Instead, He spoke to them about working together and even bearing the punishment and consequences of their sin as a couple. Yes, there were parts of the curse that affected their ability to walk in their god-ordained roles without trying to usurp one another but He kept them together for better and worse.

When He removed them from the garden, God didn't single Adam out by sending him off because of his failed responsibility in protecting his family from the lies and deceit of the serpent or because of his failure to hold the family to God's standard after Eve had been tempted.

He also didn't send Eve out of Eden without Adam for her part in listening to the serpent's lies and temptation, but they were both given equal responsibility in the sin that had taken place and it's consequences.

God never desires to see marriages broken. What God has joined together, He admonishes that no man (or woman) should separate. This shows us the heavy weight He places on this covenant. Not even sin is meant to separate the two of you. This bond is lifelong and exclusive.

Unbelieving Spouse?

Some of you may read this and exclude yourself. You may believe that because your husband or wife is not a Christian, God does not want you to be with them as that would make you unequally yoked with an unbeliever. That is not a correct interpretation of what the bible says.

When the bible talked about being "unequally yoked" it was a serious admonition intended for those who were not yet "yoked" or as we would say, "hitched"! That statement is something that should have been considered before you got married.

If you got saved after marriage you can't undo your marriage covenant now and base your reasoning on it. The bible has a clear response for those in this situation -

And if a woman has a husband who is not a believer and he is
willing to live with her, she must not divorce him.
1 Corinthian 7:13

To date, marriage and the family unit remains the most important institution of human society. It has been the backbone of human civilization and the bedrock for building a stable society. And it will continue to be so until Jesus returns.

MARRIAGE FROM GOD'S PERSPECTIVE
A Demonstration Of Unity

In Genesis 2:24, God ordained that a man would leave his father and mother, and cleave to his wife so that they would be one. So in God's plan for marriage, we are to leave all else and come together as one just like God the Father, the Holy Spirit and his son Jesus Christ are one. Therefore marriage is intended to demonstrate this level of oneness of heart and unity.

A Suitable Helper

At the time that God had only created man, He gave him charge of the garden and told him he could eat from every tree in the garden but he should not eat from the Tree of the Knowledge of Good and Evil. Then He called him and said "it is not good that [he] should be alone". He wanted to give Adam a helper so He passed all the animals in front of him to see which of them would suit him.

The man gave names to all the cattle, and to the birds of the sky, and to every beast of the field, but for Adam there was not found a helper suitable for him.
Genesis 2:20

God had passed every single animal in front of Adam to see which of them will be sufficient in administering the assistance and help that he was going to need for the assignment God had for him. Adam named all the cattle, the birds of the air, every beast of the field, but the Bible says that there was no helper comparable or suitable to him.

> *Marriage is intended to demonstrate the same level of oneness of heart and unity that is between the Trinity.*

So the Lord caused a deep sleep to fall on Adam and He took one of his ribs and closed up the flesh in its place. And God used the rib which he had taken from man to make the woman and he brought her to the man. Now Adam said when he saw her, *"this is the bone of my bones, and the flesh of my flesh. She will be called woman because she was taken out of man."* Genesis 2:23

From this we can see that God wanted to provide a helper for the man, a united team to do what He had called them to on the earth, together.

Leave and Cleave

It was also in this context that God said, *"therefore a man will leave his father and mother and be joined to his wife and they will become one flesh".*

Adam and Eve didn't have a father and mother to leave in order to cleave to one another. God was their Father. Yet He knew that you (Mr. and Mrs.) would be coming after them and would have an obligation to your fathers and your mothers before you get married. So He made it clear that when you choose marriage, your primary obligation shifts.

You leave your father and mother and are joined together with your spouse and you both become one flesh. Note that they were both naked and yet the man and his wife and were not ashamed, see Chapter Ten on sex.

It is interesting that in Western culture, it's normally the woman who physically leaves her family but the instruction to leave and cleave is given to the man. He was not making a mistake. Some people think of leaving and cleaving as a physical act of moving away from one's parents and moving into your husband's house or having your wife move in with you. Leaving and cleaving is not just physical, it is a spiritual and mental exercise.

For some men it's really difficult to leave their mothers and cleave to their wives. You use your mother as a comparison of what you expect from your wife. "She can't cook like her", "She can't clean like her". This is a grave mistake. Afterall, if your mother was such a wonderful woman, why didn't you stay in her house? You chose this person over your mother, so now mentally, with your tastebuds, leave your mother and cleave to your wife.

To Have Dominion

We also see here that it was after God gave Adam his wife that he gave him the command to dominate the Earth.

God created man in His own image, in the image of God He created him…
Genesis 1:27(a)

Now based on Genesis 2, we see that there was a pause in this conversation. He passed the animals before man, and only after that, do we continue with the second half of verse 27.

…male and female He created them. Gen 1:27(b)

After He had created male and female, what did He do?

God blessed them; and God said to them, "Be fruitful and multiply, and fill the earth, and subdue it; and rule over the fish of the sea and over the birds of the sky and over every living thing that moves on the earth."
Then God said, "Behold, I have given you every plant yielding seed that is on the surface of all the earth, and every tree which has fruit yielding seed; it shall be food for you;
Genesis 1:28-29

Therefore, this is your first and primary divine commitment. Your first commandment from God within the context of marriage. To be fruitful, multiply and fill the earth. Subdue it. Have dominion and bring the very kingdom of God to the earth, as it is in heaven.

Through this passage you can see a foundational outline of God's purpose for marriage and as you continue throughout His word, He reveals many different aspects of what your marriage is to look like.

A godly marriage will have the fruit of His kingdom in it, which is righteousness, peace and joy in the Holy Spirit. When your marriage is godly, there is peace and there is joy.

Everything may not be perfect, but the sanctuary that is within the home remains stable through the storms of life.

God's divine purpose for marriage is to show His glory, for childbearing and to provide you with companionship and physical intimacy.

THE PURPOSE OF MARRIAGE
Marriage Was Created For The Glory Of God

When God asked Adam and Eve to be fruitful and multiply, fill the Earth and subdue it, remember that He had created them "in his own image" (vs 27). So as they multiplied, it wasn't just for the fun of it. They were not just having children for the sake of having children. And neither are you.

You are not just married for the sake of gaining possessions, or making your family's name great. You have been created in the image of God, you have been given divine DNA and He put you here so that you can multiply His image on the earth.

Giving birth to children is not enough. Are you multiplying a God-awareness in and through them? Not having children is also not a reason to step back from this command from God. Are you teaching others how to subdue the earth and have dominion? Are you producing fruit in the lives of people around you through your marriage and individual lives?

You have to see the big picture. When Adam and Eve disobeyed God in Eden, they relinquished the dominion and authority that He had given to them on earth and handed it over to the serpent. Yet before they ever fell, God had purposed that this same man who was made in His image, would have His authority on the earth. That you would be the one to speak His word and watch it multiplied and established.

> *Your marriage is able to highlight the truth, worth, beauty and greatness of God.*

When the devil succeeded in stealing this authority from man, God sent his son Jesus Christ as a man on the earth to reclaim our dominion and He did just that!

Jesus Christ regained what Adam and Eve lost. So now, based on the work that Jesus Christ did through His death and resurrection, you have access to the same authority that God gave Adam and Eve. Your marriage is able to highlight the truth, worth, beauty and greatness of God. Your marriage can and should show His power, providence, mercy, wisdom, grace, riches, love and authority.

ACTION POINTS:

Pray and ask God and each other the following questions:

- What does this look like for you? How can you walk in the authority Jesus has won for you as a couple?
- What is the primary focus of your marriage?
- Do you see your marriage in light of the purposes of God or has it been all about "us" and what we want?
- What does being fruitful, multiplying, subduing the earth and having dominion over it look like between you and your spouse?
- What specific calling or passion has God placed in the both of you, not just for your family, but for your community and the world at large?

Marriage is a spiritual undertaking. It is a partnership where you place the interests of your spouse and children above yourself – a relationship that ultimately mirrors God's sacrificial love toward each of us.

Marriage Was Created For Companionship

Marriage was created for companionship. It was created so that you would have and give to your spouse company, assistance with life matters, accountability and a constant prayer partner.

Company

In Genesis 2:18, God's observation was not that Adam was alone physically, but that he was lonely. He had the company of animals and birds, but could not communicate with them. If you look from an eternal perspective, you will see that the portion of time in which you are married to each other is relatively very short. Even if you get to eighty years of marriage, it is much less than the billions of years our souls will be satisfied and filled with joy in the presence of God. Yet for this short time, it is helpful to have company as you go through the challenges, joys, and myriads of experiences that come with life on earth.

Companionship is deeper than being in the same space. Looking at marriage through the lens of companionship is seeing it as a friendship. It is having a person you can walk through life with. A friend you can confide in. A friend you can share the deepest parts of your life with. Someone that you can run ideas by. It's a place of knowing one another more than anyone else in the world. Sharing your dreams, goals, hobbies, conversation, joy, prayers and tears.

There's nothing worse than being married and lonely. Like Mary Ann Shaffer said - "I don't want to be

> *There's nothing worse than being married and lonely.*

married just to be married. I can't think of anything lonelier than spending the rest of my life with someone I can't talk to, or worse, someone I can't be silent with."

Companionship is comfort in shared silence. Being able to be in the same room, know that your spouse is there, completely silent and yet feel together. Companionship is giving each other hugs regularly. It is sharing a quick kiss before or after putting the children to sleep or before going out to work. It is sharing the events of your day no matter how mundane with your spouse.

Marriage is meant to alleviate loneliness and provide companionship.

Assistance With Life Matters

Marriage is also assisting each other, nurturing, caring, affirming and guiding one another. Assistance with life matters is a practical thing to give and receive.

Sitting down together to discuss what your immediate, short and long term goals are and how you want to achieve them. Discussing and building a plan around what the ultimate purpose of your lives is. How do you want to be remembered? What legacy are you leaving on this earth?

Or light things, like having someone to sit, watch TV, and take rest with after getting worn out from work. Taking turns changing your children's diapers. Each of you pitching in to cover the bills and rent. A godly marriage is a place of rest, a place of joy.

> *"Sometimes the most ordinary things could be made extraordinary, simply by doing them with the right people."*
> *Nicholas Sparks*

Accountability

What the closest people around you see and know of you is a lot of times the true indicator of your character. There are too many individuals who think that their ministry is what earns them a place before God. They totally disregard and sometimes even abuse their families and don't understand that your marriage and family life is one of the primary places God searches and knows you.

Your marriage is a place where your spouse can show you things in yourself that you wouldn't have seen otherwise, areas in your character that need adjustment. They can also encourage you in what you have improved in over the years as they have watched you grow.

ACTION POINT:

Husbands and wives take a break right now and...

* Encourage your spouse in areas of growth you have seen in their lives over the years.
* Tell them at least one thing they have improved on in their character, way of thinking or behaviour since you have been married.

Your spouse is the person that will best remember where you used to be weak and see where those weaknesses have become strengths. Your spouse can also help to remind you of God's faithfulness to both of you in times when you get tired of believing.

He or she will (or should) help you realize when your talk has become louder than your walk. They can check you when your character is out of line in a conversation and no one else wants to mention it to you. Oh! And they are always the best person to point out the green leaf of spinach in your teeth when no one else will. So embrace this place of accountability. Enjoy it and help each other become better people.

"It doesn't matter how holy you are outside your home, what matters most is what your wife (or husband) and children think of you in the privacy of your home."
Amos Dada

Prayer Partner

Lastly but certainly not least in the area of companionship, God has given you a life-long prayer partner in your spouse. Someone with whom you can share your deepest fears, hopes, dreams, and together come before God to pray accordingly.

Again I say to you, that if two of you agree on earth about anything that they may ask, it shall be done for them by My Father who is in heaven. Matthew 18:19

That my friend, is powerful. God gives you a blank check, complete access within your marriage to ask Him for anything - according to His will - and watch it come to pass. Do not forfeit this opportunity to create a journey with your spouse, tracking the prayers you pray and God's gracious responses to them. Marriage was made for this.

Agree on earth.

Watch it take place.

Give the glory back to God.

Therefore, confess your sins to one another and pray for one another, that you may be healed. The prayer of a righteous person has great power as it is working.

James 5:16

You can see that God ordained marriage for His glory, your companionship, assistance with life matters, accountability and in order to give you a life long prayer partner, but that gift He has given you will only be as good as you make it. Now we will look at another purpose that God had in mind when He instituted marriage, intimacy.

Marriage Was Created To Allow A Godly Physical Expression Of Love - Intimacy

There is a longing in many of us for this sort of unification with another human being. A desire to be held, touched, and one with another. This "eros" love is not an evil desire but has been placed in you by God Himself. Eros love is the physical, sensual intimacy between husband and wife. It expresses sexual and romantic attraction.

It is a God-given gift to husbands and wives to build a level of unity, and friendship that is exclusive only to your union. All other types of love can be shared between the two of you, and also between you and your children, friends, relatives etc. but not eros. Eros is reserved for the private honourable space of your marriage bed. And it was set up this way intentionally.

Nevertheless, to avoid sexual immorality, let every man have his
own wife, and let every woman have her own husband.
1 Corinthians 7:2

Paul also later instructed people within the Corinthian church to get married lest they "burn" with passion. Some think that getting married soon after an engagement is a "cop out" from fighting lust head on, yet this is part of what God prescribes as an appropriate response to feeling overwhelmed by the desire to have sex. Especially when you already know that you plan on getting married. Paul instructed them to get married so that they could have that intimate closeness and avoid fornication.

> *Your marriage is a context where there is no guilt or shame attached to the act of sex.*

Your marriage is the context where there is no guilt or shame attached to the act of sex. It is an act of pure, holy worship, just like singing in church is. With this said however, no one should get married just for the purpose of having sex as you probably know by now, that sex is just one part of your married life.

Marriage is also designed for purity after your wedding day and during the latter parts of your lives. We are under assault from various sexual temptations from many directions. From practically naked men and women on billboards and magazines at the grocery stores. Advertisements that promote lust more than they do products and services, to television shows that feature enough skin and sexual content to qualify them as soft pornography, to unwanted pornographic pop ups while you are checking your email.

The enemy is working overtime trying to draw many men and women into a life of sexual sin and the bond of marriage gives you the needed support to defeat that temptation by engaging in deep, satisfying love right at home. A love that gives to, and receives from, your spouse physically, emotionally, and spiritually.

"It is good for a man not to touch a woman. Nevertheless, because of sexual immorality, let each man have his own wife, and let each woman have her own husband. Let the husband render to his wife the affection due her, and likewise also the wife to her husband. The wife does not have authority over her own body, but the husband does. And likewise the husband does not have authority over his own body, but the wife does. Do not deprive one another except with consent for a time, that you may give yourselves to fasting and prayer; and come together again so that Satan does not tempt you because of your lack of self-control."
1 Corinthians 7:1-5

Here, it is clear that God is not against sex, in fact He has instituted marriage as the space where it is completely acceptable by Him. He is also making it very clear that the sex in marriage is to be between the husband and his own wife and that they are not to deprive one another.

So marriage is physical in that there is a coming together and when this takes place, it produces. It bears fruit. Yourself and your spouse though separate biological beings blend together to create what neither of you can create on your own: children.

Marriage Was Created For Childbearing

Another reason God ordained marriage is for childbearing. Genesis 1:24-31 tells us that after God created Adam and Eve, He commanded them to populate the world. God's plan was not to revisit creation after the first seven days. In fact we can see that he had created each tree, plant, and animal with the mechanisms they needed to reproduce after their own kind (seeds etc).

And God blessed them; and God said to them, "Be fruitful and multiply, and fill the earth, and subdue it; and rule over the fish of the sea and over the birds of the sky, and over every living thing that moves on the earth." (NASB) Genesis 1:28

His intention was not to continue to form men out of dust, breathing His breath of life into them as He did with Adam. Instead in His amazing, incomprehensible wisdom and plan, He created within both man and woman, yourself and your spouse everything needed for you to do what He did. Create. He is the Master designer and His ways are without searching. They are beyond us.

Can You Imagine The Glory Of God In Childbearing?

The forming of another human from the simple union of the egg and sperm of a man and woman. An embryo that begins as one cell, and independently begins to form everything needed for life on earth.

Can you imagine a baby in the womb who at a gestational age of five weeks, though he/she is less than one quarter of an inch, already has their brain, spinal cord and heart development underway. A specific God ordained process where at exactly five weeks and one day, their heart begins to beat and is visible in an ultrasound. A baby that is able to respond to touch by fifteen weeks in the womb! Too many times the wonders of God in this privilege of bearing children He has given to mankind is overlooked.

> *Too many times the wonders of God in this privilege of bearing children He has given to mankind is overlooked.*

This calling, this mandate from heaven to be fruitful and multiply is not just physical but spiritual. Even married couples who are yet to bear physical children are able to set as a vision for their marriage the spiritual multiplication of what God has deposited in them. God expects your marriage to produce godly fruit within others, sometimes in those that are your own age mates or older. To pour the life of God into another human, to disciple and mentor others in a focused way. Godly marriages are able to take on the mentorship of young men and women showing them what healthy relationships look like.

When a marriage produces a child, or receives a child through adoption, it is one of life's greatest blessings. Roughly forty percent of children being raised today are in a home without a father. The effects of that fact are staggering. The absence of fathers has been proven to lead to increases in mental and behavioural disorders as well as criminal activity and substance abuse. But when children are raised inside a healthy marriage, they get front row seats to see and experience the lasting benefits of a strong family.

This is not to condemn homes where this could not be helped but to highlight the need for you to fight for your marriages. This is also said to highlight the opportunity for godly christian men to be fathers to the fatherless. For women to mentor those who are younger than them in the ways of God. For both of you to be open and willing to physically adopt children (even if you have your own already) so that they have the opportunity to grow up in homes that are full of the love of Christ and to see that they are precious and wanted.

Marriage is meant to provide emotional and financial security for the children in the home. When a child feels secure within their own home, their character and personality will have a good foundation to weather unfavourable external influences. But if they are deprived of that, their development is in great danger of being warped and distorted and opens the door to a lack of identity which can become a higher challenge and obstacle to overcome as they grow older.

Divided homes never "just happen", they usually start with a neglect of the purpose of marriage and a misunderstanding of its definition.

WHAT MARRIAGE IS NOT

There are many who see nothing wrong with polygamous and/or "open" marriages where both spouses are free to have sexual relations outside of their marriage. This defiles the marriage bed and makes it dishonourable. It is not God's intended plan for marriage and it is adultery.

Also, marriage is not cohabitation. Though our society may render such situations "common law" marriages and sanction it by law, a marriage that God recognizes is one that has been brought before Him through some form of formal agreement to commit to one another. It can be a state marriage such as what is done in the court, or a traditional, or religious ceremony as long as it is a clear statement of the commitment of both parties to love one another and honour one another as their partner for life. This includes the consummation of that marriage.

Finally

This book is not going to detail to you what your spouse needs to begin or stop, but encourage you to begin to build the marriage you desire to have. The responsibility falls a hundred percent at your feet just as it does a hundred percent at the feet of your spouse. Your marriage is what you make of it.

For a marriage to succeed, you need to understand the roles of the man and woman. You see, though man and woman are equal as God's children, they are created with important differences that allow them to give themselves and to receive each other as a gift.

These differences though a blessing, can become the very challenges that shake and even break a marriage if they are not acknowledged and dealt with properly. We will begin to examine the roles of each spouse in your marriage and for this discussion we will start with the head of the home, the Mr.

3

The Role Of The Husband

*Women were created from the rib of man to be beside him,
not from his head to top him, nor from his feet to be trampled
by him, but from under his arm to be protected by him, near
to his heart to be loved by him.*

—MATTHEW HENRY

God has a specific place for the husband. You have been given a high privilege and you have to understand what He expects of you in order to give your one hundred percent into having a strong, lasting and happy marriage. In God's order, you give leadership, have a duty to provide for your family and have the joy of loving your wife.

*"Wives, submit to your husbands, as is fitting in the Lord.
Husbands, love your wives and do not be harsh with them"*

Colossians 3:18-19

Here, God highlights two fundamental and immutable spiritual principles that will give your marriage relationship the surest foundation for lasting joy.

The first is 'Husbands love your wives'.

The second, 'Wives submit to your husbands'.

From these verses we see that love and respect characterize both of your roles. When these are present, then authority, headship, love, and submission will be no problem for either of you. Of course it would be beneficial for you both to love one another in order for your marriage to last, but it's interesting that the Bible does not say to the Mrs., "Love your husband!" Instead, the challenge to love is a clear command God gives to the Mr.

I believe that's because the expression and emotion of love come more naturally to women and is sometimes difficult for men to show expressions of love. Especially men who have never witnessed this being done or live in a culture where affection for your wife is not celebrated.

Mr., understand that one of your wife's most fundamental cravings is for affection. She wants to know that you love her! She wants to be treated with fondness, tenderness, warmth and caring physical attention in and outside of the home (and the bedroom).

What Does Love Look Like Within Marriage?

Love itself is very complex to define but Paul helps us in this area.

Love is patient,
Love is kind and is not jealous;
Love does not brag and is not arrogant,

It does not act unbecomingly;
It does not seek its own,
Is not provoked,
Does not take into account a wrong suffered,
Love does not rejoice in unrighteousness, but rejoices with the truth;
Love bears all things, believes all things, hopes all things, endures
all things.
1 Cor 13:4-7 NASB

In fact, Ephesians 5:28-29 exhorts men to love their wives in the same way they love their own bodies, feeding and caring for them. A man's love for his wife should be the same as Christ's love for His body, the Church.

Christ loved us with compassion, mercy, forgiveness, respect, and selflessness. He didn't wait for you to have all your tee's crossed and your i's dotted. To have perfect character, habits and thoughts, but instead, He loved you so much that He died in your place - while you were totally against Him. That is how He expects you to love your wife.

You may be thinking, "I do love my wife." "I love her with all my heart." "She should know that I do, look at how hard I work to provide for the family." But does she know it? Have you learned how to express your love to her in a way that she can understand and receive it? Or do you assume that she is reading your mind and just "knows"?

Does She Know You Love Her?

Here's the thing. If you are expressing love to your wife in a way that is different from how she understands and receives it, it is going over her head! You may be working hard to show her you love her - in the way you normally receive love, but if it isn't what she is looking for, you are missing the mark. While you are expressing your love by working hard, she may be growing more and more distant from you wondering if you even care about her because she is looking for your time or a small inexpensive gift.

I also want the Mrs. to listen up for how you can share love with your husband in a way that he is will receive it.

In so many families, the husband loves his wife and children and he shows it by working hard to provide for them. He goes out from morning until nighttime, working and earning enough money for a nice house, food on the table and beautiful clothes. While he is doing that, they are missing their father and husband and wondering if he isn't around because he does not enjoy them.

If your wife thoroughly enjoys receiving gifts, and wants you to give her things, then by all means, work hard and get those things she loves. But if she would much rather you spend some quality time with her, decide (together) what your basic needs are, then instead of climbing the corporate ladder, and aiming for the nicer house in the nicer area with the nicer stuff, spend extra time with her. This sort of wife will be much happier with your time than with the more expensive gifts you have to offer.

Here's a side note for the Mrs. You can't get it all. If you want your husband to provide all the top name brands, lavish jewelry etc you can't complain that he spends all his time trying to earn the money for the gifts that suit your expensive taste. He cannot do it all. Figure out what your top priorities are and be willing to meet him where he is.

When your expression of love matches the way that she

receives it, she is a happy, thriving woman. When she can be secure knowing that she is the apple of your eye, cherished above all others, she will be willing to follow you anywhere you lead her. She will be confident that whatever decisions you are making are what you think are the best for herself and the rest of the family.

At this point you're probably wondering, how on earth do I express love to my wife in the way that is unique to her? It's easy. Notice what things make her melt more than others. I'll share with you a couple of different types of expressions of love and you can look at each one, talk to her and determine which of them she really appreciates. Then focus more on expressing love to her in that specific way. It is worthy to note that the way she experiences love can also change in different seasons of life.

Your Words Matter

When we were younger we used to sing a song that said, 'Sticks and stones may break my bones but words can never hurt me'. We have grown up to find out how untrue and unscriptural that was. Words can kill and words can give life physically, emotionally psychologically and spiritually.

Death and life are in the power of the tongue: and they that love
it shall eat the fruit thereof.
Proverbs 18: 21

With your words, you are able to build her up to do things she didn't know she was capable of. You are able to comfort and encourage her when she feels worn out and tired. Both of you should keep in mind that encouraging your spouse is not about using words to try to get him/her to do what you want. It's using your words to help them do what they want or need to do.

Husband, it's choosing to use your words to make her smile, even if she thinks you're silly for doing it. Turn to her before going to bed and say - "You are the best gift God has given me in this world." At random times in the day remind her of why you married her in the first place.

Here are some examples of things you can say to your wife to show her you love her. I know this really does not come naturally to all of you and for others, you may have started your marriage saying many of these things but have forgotten them.

Words For Your Wife

Use them often.
- "I love you"
- "You are so beautiful"
- "You are just amazing"
- "I appreciate _____"
- "You make that dress come alive"
- "You make me smile"
- "There's no one I'd rather come home to/spend my day with"
- "Thank you for _____"
- "Wow what you cooked today was special"
- "I am sorry"
- "Forgive me"
- "I can't believe you did all this after coming home from work, WOW! Thank you darling!"

Therefore encourage one another and build up each other, just as you are in fact doing.
1 Thessalonians 5:11

Challenge yourself to give her at least one compliment everyday. You appreciate her, let her know with your words and make it fun! If she does something amazing, tell her.

If you are really annoyed by her and your marriage has come to a point where she cannot seem to do anything good, take an objective step back from the situation and look for the good in her. Begin to speak and highlight it. Your words may come as a surprise to her, but be assured over time, she will begin to believe you and your focus on the good will amplify the good in her.

For some reason, in some African cultures it is seen as weakness to admit love. As though it makes a man vulnerable and that vulnerability is not "masculine". I beg you, for the sake of your marriage, forget about that nonsense and tell your wife you love her. Let others call it weakness or say you are less of a man for it. You get to strengthen your own marriage and preserve it. Like that family I mentioned earlier, you are choosing to "live your own life" and let them live theirs. And for you Mrs., as your husband picks this back up, apply what I say in "Accepting His Love" (Chapter Four).

Lastly, as we speak about your words, don't shout at your wife, accuse her constantly or put her down. Don't compare your wife to another woman, particularly not to your mother or her mother. After all, you didn't marry her mother, or your own mother. You chose to marry her.

Love Is An Action

"Husbands, love your wives, just as Christ loved the church and gave himself up for her to make her holy, cleansing her by the washing with water through the word"
Ephesians 5:25-26

Husbands, don't just love your wife with words, show her practically. Some of you are telling your wife how much you love and appreciate her and she is thinking "if only you would help me out." Especially if your wife receives love through acts of service, take the time to serve her.

Look for ways to assist her around the house. Start with some chores you know absolutely frustrate her, something she has mentioned she dreads doing. Listen to her. Wash the dishes, take out the garbage. Fry plantain or make a full dinner one day. Hold the car door open for her to get in. Get the children ready for school. Watch the children while she goes out with her friends for an evening. Watch the children while she goes out for a walk by herself.

I remember a day I had worked all day and was exhausted. I came home and my husband had cooked up a full dinner. The children had to help him for some parts of it but it was such an amazing feeling to know he cared enough to step out of his comfort zone in that way.

Once my husband wanted to cook to give me a break and ended up pouring our dishwashing liquid soap in the frying pan thinking it was the oil. Himself and the children knew something was wrong when the "oil" started to bubble out of the pan. It must be a "guy" thing because years later my son-in-law did the exact same thing while wanting to fry plantain for my husband at our house.

As you can imagine, we had a very good laugh about it. Mrs., when your husband messes up the laundry folding and puts things in the wrong place, don't get mad about it. Be grateful that he tried to help you! If you curse and ridicule him, he will not be helping you again.

Serve Joyfully!

I have a friend who would list out every way her assistance to me was an inconvenience to her. It sucked the joy out of receiving the gift. What's the point of giving and doing for your wife, if you tell her how much you hate it? Be a cheerful server.

In most African cultures, it is primarily the wife's role to cook, clean and take care of the children and home. In the twenty-first century, this is coupled with an expectation that she is also working a full-time job to assist in the family's finances. This can get overwhelming and stressful. Understand that she isn't superhuman. She cannot do it all alone. Split the workload so that things are not solely falling on her shoulders. She is your wife, not your house maid.

> "My little children, let us not love in word or in tongue, but in deed and in truth."
> 1 John 3:18.

What if you also hate doing those chores (or any chore at all)? Choose to help her out anyway and do it with a smile. Love gives sacrificially and if you start doing it faithfully and you'll get better at it over time. Before you know, it will become a habit that you don't even think about and she will love you over the moon and back for it.

I am going to confess to you both. I have a bad habit

of cooking up amazing meals, doing many different types of dishes at the same time without packing it all up and putting it away. I just don't enjoy that part. We all know that if you don't put your food away on time, it will go bad. But like clockwork even when I least expect it, my darling husband will get up long after I have gone to bed, notice the pots of food on the stove and put it all away. How do you think that makes me feel when I wake up? I am sure the Mrs. would love to see some of those random acts of kindness within the house. Cover for her weaknesses instead of getting angry and throwing them in her face.

Give Her Gifts

For some of you, what makes your wife feel most loved is receiving a gift. Gifts don't have to be expensive to be given. The power of a gift is that it tells your wife you were thinking of her in the moment that you got or made it.

For example, if you are doing the groceries (an act of service), get her favorite type of nuts or chocolate bar. Don't forget her birthday. Gift her some time at the spa. Remember that some gifts don't even need to be bought. Write her a love letter like you used to before you got married (or write her one because you dated after the internet revolution and only wrote to each other through emails). There's just something about knowing that your husband went out of his way to spend time thinking about how to make you smile that… makes you smile.

Whenever you go on a trip out of the city or country, get her a small gift. This one thing makes me look forward to seeing my husband, when he comes back from his many trips. Aside from the joy of having him back, I am absolutely positive he is going to bring me something from that country or city. He knows I love to collect mugs from foreign countries, and while some people would consider that a silly hobby, he brings me my mug even when he gets me a different gift as well.

So Mr., get out a pen and paper and jot down some of the things you've noticed about her recently, ask her what she really likes or leave her a few notes all over the house in unexpected places that say things like - "hey darling, I'm thinking of you." If receiving gifts is the primary way your wife receives love, go out of your way to give her small (and big) gifts. She will love you the more for it!

Spend Some Quality Time

I hear husbands say things like, "What more does she want from me?! I work like a slave to give her a good house, she has a brand-new car and I even threw in a vacation with the kids. What else is she looking for?" She may just want time alone with you.

To be honest, a lot of men (and women) can become obsessed with work, money and financial gain. When this happens, you end up losing the very family you are working to provide for. Mr., I can promise you, it will not be worth it. No amount of vacations, pay raises or corporate promotion is worth losing your family. To them, your presence is often appreciated more than your presents.

Once I went to visit a young lady to share a business proposal with her. She lived in a massive, beautiful house with her daughter. It was such an impressive, well-kept house that I complimented her on it. To my amazement, she burst into tears. She said to me, "I hate this house! All I want is my husband. He is never here. He travels from one business trip to the other. I am alone and lonely and I feel like just another piece of furniture in the house." Wow. That highlighted this point to me all over again.

> *Your possessions and or children cannot take your place in your wife's heart. She didn't choose to marry them, she chose you.*

Your possessions and/or children cannot take your place in your wife's heart. After all she didn't choose to marry them, she chose you. They cannot fill her need for companionship, only you can.

For some of you, the problem is that even the time you spend at home is spent apart from each other. You are living like co-tenants. Texting others, being on the computer while in the house is not being engaged with each other. Keep your phone on silent in a different room and focus on the gift God has given you in your wife. Have eye contact while you speak to each other. Ask questions, comment on the "gist" and stories she has to tell you about her day. Listen and really hear her, follow up on matters that she mentioned she was concerned about beforehand. Talk to her about that co-worker that keeps nagging her at work. How is she handling it? Has it gotten better?

If this is what your spouse loves, find out what type of quality time is most valuable to him or her. For your wife, it may be to have the phones and television off to have the right atmosphere, while for others, it may be time spent watching a movie together. Either way, don't just serve her or give her gifts if all she is waiting for, is for you to sit together and play a simple game of scrabble.

Physical Touch

Dear husbands... you're married! It's ok to kiss! It's ok to be physically affectionate! Some people are so used to the correct teaching that sex outside of marriage is wrong, that they built boundaries while courting or in their engagement season to keep from having sex and forget to bring those boundaries down after they got married.

Physical touch can make or break a relationship. It can communicate hatred or love. Does your wife often reach out to touch your arm while you talk? Or does she like to greet you with a hug and a kiss instead of a simple wave goodbye as she leaves for work?

If your wife loves physical touch, sit beside her when you are together in the room. Greet her in the morning with a kiss. Don't wait until you want to have sex to follow her around the house buttering her up. It doesn't have to be a sexual thing, just a physical acknowledgment that you see her and you love her. A pat on the back, a gentle massage on her shoulders as you walk past makes a difference and will bring a smile to her face.

The How Matters

Love makes requests and not demands. When you start to make demands from your wife, you make her the child and you the parent whereas in a healthy marriage, you are equal adult partners. It is important to express your desires, but ensure that they are expressed in a way that honours and loves her. Wives, this also applies to you. The way you ask for assistance can make it a resentful task for your husband. Ask in a way that he sees where you are coming from and is more willing to gladly assist you.

Men, make sure that she is meeting your requests out of love and not from a place of fear. There should be no room for fear. Love is a choice. It cannot be forced or coerced.

Everyone has a love tank and as time passes, the tendency is for it to get lower and lower. You have the powerful opportunity to refill your wife's love tank throughout the days and years of your marriage. It may seem cumbersome, but this is what you signed up for when you said "I do" and it should be a joy. See John 15:13.

If all of this seems impossible, or too high a standard, it is not. It takes knowing God's love to love like He does. You cannot love your wife in your own power. You cannot "will" it into your consistent actions. If you need to grow in this area, read and meditate on the fourth chapter of 1st John and ask God for the grace to love.

Love is a Decision not a Feeling

I know a young man whose wife is often quite abusive in her language, will not engage in sexual intimacy and shows him clear acts of rebellion that generate strife. He would go out of his way to try to make her happy and serve herself and her family without a hint of bitterness. On seeing their relationship for some time, I asked him how he is able to show her so much love while she is blatantly unwilling to submit. I know many men would use that as their excuse for acting in a rough way toward her or allowing it to build a rift in the marriage wide enough to break the marriage apart.

> *"Love has nothing to do with what you are expecting to get—only with what you are expecting to give—which is everything."*
> —Katharine Hepburn

His response was that he was committed to loving her despite what she was doing. He said "I have decided to do what Jesus says I should do, no matter the circumstances. I am praying that she will understand that what she is doing is not right and repent, because I really love her. I reach out to her family to show her the extent of my love."

LOVE IS NOT THE END

Though love is a key ingredient to establish a lasting marriage relationship, it is not the only ingredient. God has given you some other critical roles to fulfill as a husband.

For the husband is the head of the wife as Christ is the head of the church, his body, of which he is the Savior.
Ephesians 5:23

You are to take on leadership in your home. This leadership should not be dictatorial, condescending, or patronizing, but should be in line with the example of Christ leading the church.

Be willing to make decisions with obedience to God and the strengthening of your marriage, family and community in mind. When the family is at a crossroads, listen to your wife's opinion, and prayerfully make a decision. Do not leave your family in limbo. Make it clear to them what your overall family priorities and values are, then make life choices consistent with those values. Remember to create those family values together.

Spiritual Leadership

The Lord expects you to provide spiritual leadership. This is in studying and sharing the word of God, in the place of prayer, attending church and being an active part of a godly, Christian community. Leadership in faith and trusting in God.

This is an area where you can only lead by example. "Do what I say and not what I do" will not cut it. Your family follows what you do. If you do not take this particular place of leadership, it opens the door for the enemy to create confusion and rebellion.

Being the spiritual leader does not mean that you need to have all the answers for every challenge you encounter as a family. Be willing to admit when you're stuck and don't know what to do about a situation. Share the things that burden you with your wife so that you can pray together. Remember that Jesus is your Head as you are her head.

Make prayer, bible reading and family devotional time a priority. If no one else brings it up, you do so. Your children (or wife) may complain but they will thank you for it later. Remember, "the family that prays together, stays together". Ensure that this time is not usurped by social media. There is a time for everything. Facebook and Instagram have their moments, but when it's time to pray, it's time to pray.

Servant Leadership

Jesus said that the greatest leaders are the servants of all. Choose to serve your family. Serve in love and humility. Do not lord your leadership over your wife or children.

And Jesus called them to him and said to them, "You know that those who are considered rulers of the Gentiles lord it over them, and their great ones exercise authority over them. But it shall not be so among you. But whoever would be great among you must be your servant, and whoever would be first among you must be slave of all."
Mark 10:42-44 (ESV)

Learn to apologize and own it when you are wrong. Don't give an air of infallibility, or perfection. You're human too and it is ok to make mistakes. We've already talked about assisting your wife through acts of service because you are motivated by love, now servant leadership asks the same thing from you.

If she is bathing the children, help with breakfast. When she comes home from work tired, take the initiative to make dinner. Many times my husband will say, "Iyawo (his nickname for me) please go and lay down I have taken care of myself. Do you want anything?" Your wife will be less stressed and worn out when you would like her to focus on some other physical matters that matter to both of you.

Provide Financially

In the home, the Bible instructs husbands to provide for their families. This means he works or serves in a way that earns enough money to provide at least the basic necessities of life for his wife and children. To fail to do so has definite spiritual and natural consequences.

If anyone does not provide for his relatives, and especially for his immediate family, he has denied the faith and is worse than an unbeliever.

1 Timothy 5:8

A man who makes no effort to provide for his family cannot call himself a Christian. This does not mean that she cannot assist in supporting the family, see Proverbs 31, but it is not her primary responsibility. It is yours and she needs that financial security even if she does not say so.

It also doesn't mean that a man who is trying to find a job and has not found one is not a Christian. Life happens, and sometimes being able to provide financially for your family is out of your hands. Just give this one hundred percent of your effort. If you do not have a job and have high career goals, pursue those goals, but work somewhere in the meantime. Even if it has to be a "survival" job. You want your family's basic needs covered while you work towards getting that big career break.

If you serve in ministry and you do not earn a paycheck, you still need to ensure that you are planning for how your family is going to eat and pay bills. You are no longer a bachelor. You cannot say that because you are doing "the Lord's work", your wife and children should go hungry while you minister. If everyone else can ignore the "money" factor, you cannot because you have others that are dependent on you. It doesn't mean that you should stop doing ministry, but you may need to take on a part-time or relief job or help watch the children so that your wife is able to work. Whatever works best for your family.

Provide Security

First of all you are to provide her the security of a proper marriage honoured in God's sight.

For this reason a man shall leave his father and mother and be joined to his wife, and the two shall become one flesh'? So they are no longer two, but one flesh. What therefore God has joined together, let no man separate."
Matthew 19:5-6 NASB

I know two women who moved in with their boyfriends, or as they call them their "husbands" because they gave them the promise of having an official marriage later on. Many years later, that formal marriage has not taken place. Both of these women unfortunately haven't been able to forgive their partners. They feel cheated and used and the fact that they are not in a committed marriage continues to affect their overall relationship today.

When the reason for the women's deep rooted bitterness was exposed, the men could not understand what the problem was. The men's position was that they had already lived together and had children so "what is the point?" One of the couples even had some of their children get married and leave the home, so he was that much more convinced that they didn't need the formality of their own "marriage ceremony". It took the grace of God for one of those marriages to be restored while unfortunately the second marriage did not make it. So as basic and silly as it may seem, I have to highlight that your wife needs the security of a proper official marriage.

Also, a woman wants to feel secure within her marriage. Make no mistake, if you have wandering eyes, she notices. There should be no doubt in her mind that she is your one and only. Never, and I repeat, never make jokes about being with another woman, having a girlfriend on the side or getting a divorce. Even if she laughs along with you, the bitter taste of a potential truth to that joke will not leave her mouth.

> *Never make jokes about being with another woman, having a girlfriend on the side or getting a divorce.*

Use your words of affirmation to encourage her in her worth and value. Tell her she is beautiful. Especially if she has given birth to children and may not look like she did on your wedding day any longer. Who does? Don't compare her to others, allow her to be confident in the way God has created her.

Don't Be Jealous Of Your Wife

Over the years, I have met a number of men who allow themselves to become jealous of their wife's achievements. In such cases, it develops into a spirit of competition and they end up going out of their way to pull their wives down. These are men who cannot bear to see their wives receive greater accolades or do better than them. Anytime their wives achieve social, financial, academic or ministerial success, they get upset and are unable to handle it. These men don't just find it difficult to support their wives in achieving her own goals, they stand as barriers to her progress. Husbands, this is not the way a marriage should be if you want it to last and have joy.

A woman I knew many years ago worked in the banking industry, but was very gifted in making and trading home essential items like bedsheets etc. She started a side business creating and selling her home essentials and because of her level of skill, it became very lucrative. While others were celebrating her success, her husband did everything in his power to stop her business from succeeding.

He made it difficult for her to create the supplies she needed, and at a point forbade her from doing the business. When she emphasized it was for the family's good and would bring in extra income he maintained his position. His pride could not stand to watch her earn more income than he did. He consistently blamed her accomplishments for unrelated problems in their relationship and it became such a point of contention that she eventually gave up her business to make him happy. But here's the issue - he was never happy if she was making tangible progress or having success in any area of life. You can guess where that marriage ended up.

Reading this, it is easy to point the finger at him and say how can he be so blind and foolish to cut off his nose to spite his face? How could he not realize that his wife's success was his own success? But many others do the same.

ACTION POINTS

Ask yourself these questions to see if there is a hint of this prideful jealousy in you.

- Are you resentful anytime your wife has a promotion or "gets a break" in life?
- Do you go out of your way to compete against her when she succeeds in anything?
- Do you downplay her success, instead of celebrating her, are you constantly reminding her of what she has not done or her areas of weakness?
- Do you constantly brag about how she "could not have done it without [you]"?
- Do you dismiss her attempts to teach you something new or give you advice?
- Do you use her achievements as bragging rights with your friends but never tell her how great she is or what a great job she has done?

If you are genuinely committed to a happy marriage, you cannot give room to the devil in this way. It is prideful, egocentric and self-centered. You don't have to bring in the most money, have the most awards etc. That is a very limited way of thinking. You should be her biggest supporter. Remember her success is your success just like your success is hers. So rejoice in it!

If you really don't know how to change this within yourself, it needs to be a focused prayer issue. Begin to pray for her to be blessed. Give her room to grow and expand with your words. Encourage her actively. Ask questions about how her business, career or endeavours are going.

Here I will insert a note for the ladies. If you know that your husband fits these examples, don't ignore it and live in la-la land. Don't just withdraw into a shell, become an underachiever and live less than what God has placed you on the earth for. Don't give into inner hidden bitterness watching your dreams pass you by daily. Take the time to calmly and respectfully talk with your husband about how you feel in a positive productive way.

Do not walk in pride and arrogance when you are having a season of success that is more than what he is experiencing. The tables can turn at any time. Don't rub your extra income in his face with comments like "I bought that, it's mine." or "I can do anything I want, it's my money." What's his is yours, what's yours is his.

Try to see it from his perspective or at least acknowledge his feelings. Then get him involved in your story. Bring him along with you on the journey. If there are areas where your decisions will affect the family, talk to him before you make those decisions. If a promotion would affect your arrangements for child-care or his career, think it through and have reasonable solutions that work for both of you.

Your marriage is about walking together, preferring each other above yourselves, learning from your failures and celebrating your successes together.

Acknowledge Her Place As Your Wife

Show her that she has the key to your heart. Sometimes, other people (your children included) will ask her to approach you about things that you have already told them "no". Now and then, change your answer to a yes, to show them that her approaching you is different from anyone else. It is small but she will notice and appreciate that you are able to listen to her enough to change your mind on certain matters.

Safety

Husbands, love your wives and do not be bitter toward them.
Colossians 3:19

It is important to your wife that you make your home her safe haven physically, psychologically and emotionally. She should feel and be safe from both internal and external threats and fear.

This goes without saying, never abuse your wife physically, verbally or sexually. You should be her hiding place. If you have abused her in the past, do not excuse it or blame her for the abuse. Acknowledge your mistake, apologize and never repeat the behaviour. Abuse dehumanizes. There is never anything that she can do to warrant such a devalue of her person. There is never a reason to swear, hit, yell or curse at her. (Mrs, the same goes for you).

She is not your property. She is a daughter of God and should be treated as such. Too many men within the church pray long and "great" prayers and are abusing their wives at home. They have forgotten that the Lord said,

Husbands, in the same way be considerate as you live with your
wives, and treat them with respect as the weaker partner and as
heirs with you of the gracious gift of life, so that nothing will hinder
your prayers.
1 Peter 3:7 (NIV)

If you dishonour her as the weaker partner, you are hindering your own prayers. Too many men wonder why their lives seem stuck and have been unable to move forward despite their many prayers and yet daily put down their wives verbally and dishonour them before their friends, children or when nobody's watching.

There is a false belief within the Christian community that Christian men, especially those who are part of the five-

> *A man who preaches his face off but constantly puts down his wife or children is far from the truth.*

fold ministry (pastors, teachers, evangelists, apostles and prophets), or who minister or serve in anyway cannot be abusive. Especially if they are talented or anointed at what they do. This is a myth and a terrible fallacy!

A man who preaches his face off every Sunday, Wednesday, Saturday and in between but constantly puts down, yells at, hits or throws things at his wife or children is very far from the truth and his preaching will not save him. The fact is many women are too loyal or afraid to speak out, but be sure of this abuse will be exposed. It's like blowing up a balloon. One day it will reach its limit and pop. (See Chapter Seventeen for more on Abuse).

Remember, perfect love casts out fear. Love means providing mental, physical and emotional safety.

A Word For Ministers

Do not mistake your personal relationship with God for ministry. Do not put your wife after your ministry. Minister's wives are some of the loneliest people on the planet because while their husbands serve everyone else and fix other people's marriages, they come home too tired to invest quality time in their own home and marriage relationship. This should not be so.

Your wife sees you spend half an hour praying for a sister in the church for healing. Yet, when she is ill, you tell her to go and pray for herself, that she should have faith because God hears her prayers.

Whenever your ministry or work life is beginning to drain the energy needed for your relationship with your wife, cut back! What is it worth to have a church with 15,000 members and your own family is broken and torn? Prioritize your home above your ministry and God will honour you for it.

Finally

God has set up accountability for every husband in their home and it starts with your family. What your wife sees of you inside your home counts much more than what people see of you outside. It is more important than your career, church involvement, ministry, anointing, or the number of children you have.

Any man can choose to get married. But not every married man is a husband. Choose to be a good husband to your wife. It will pay dividends. A happy wife will accelerate your destiny.

4

Being A Godly, Happy Wife

Every wise woman builds her house: but the foolish plucks it down with her hands.

—KING SOLOMON

From the first day of Creation until the fifth, God reviewed the work that he did at the end of each day and declared it was "good". He did this for the trees, stars, the separation of waters, beasts of the field, birds of the air, fish of the seas and all other works. But on day six, when He created the man and the woman, He changed His vocabulary about how much he appreciated his creation and said it was "very good" (see Genesis 1:31).

Mrs, you are "very good". In fact, you are the "good thing" from Proverbs 18:22 that proves to your husband the favour of God in his life. I say this to you because it is really important that you appreciate yourself. You are an amazing creation of God. Wonderfully and beautifully made. Your value is much beyond what you understand. God did not make a mistake when He created you. You may look at your social media timelines and only see "super wives", "super moms" and other "wonder women", but you are not any less.

You are capable of greatness in the eyes of God and it starts first with being aware of the value that He has placed inside of you in the person of the Holy Spirit.

Whether you are married, single, separated or divorced, your identity in Christ does not change. Yet there are a few key words of wisdom I have to share with you that will help you walk in the role of a wife, with grace and that internal beauty that seems elusive in these days where the focus of beauty has become quite outward.

Now, most men go into marriage feeling like a million bucks. They have won the heart of the one they pursued and they are content. Yet over time, we sometimes go from being a "good thing", and a source of joy and evidence of God's favour to our husbands, to examples of the other types of wives described in the bible-

Better to live in a desert than with a quarrelsome and nagging wife.
Proverbs 21:19
It is better to live in a corner of the housetop than in a house shared with a quarrelsome wife.
Proverbs 25:24

Yikes! These are strong sentiments, that no woman wants associated with her.

So What Is The Role Of A Godly Wife?

I bet you are expecting me to say that she has to be perfect. Have it all together, all of the time. Children are obedient, food is never burned, brings in half (or more) of the family's income, all while posting perfectly made up selfies in her spotless house.

Many women have created superhuman standards for themselves as wives and mothers. These standards have become a crushing burden and have led to self-hatred, comparison, jealousy, depression, envy, covetousness and the list goes on.

So though I will be speaking of the qualities that will help your marriage and you as a wife, I want you to read with a heart willing to learn and change. Also give yourself the space needed to grow. Don't expect to become perfect at each point in one day or even a week. Focus on improving yourself as a wife, one quality at a time and God will give you the grace to reflect Him in this role.

Love Your Husbands?

We spoke in the previous chapter about the role of our husbands. The key thing the Lord says to the husband is to "love" his wife. I find it very interesting that the Lord didn't ask the wife to "love" her husband instead He asks you to submit to and respect your husband.

You may ask why this is the case, I believe it is because the emotion and actions behind "love" come a bit easier for the women whereas, showing our husbands the honour and respect that is due to them can be the greater challenge for wives. So yes, you should love your husbands and show them love in the same ways we discussed in the previous chapter however, I am going to spend more time discussing the matters that are more difficult for us as wives.

Honour and Respect

I believe that a man's self-confidence is like a balloon, if you blow it up and pop it, it will never return to the way it used to be. And it is this confidence that will allow him to lead your family well. So how do you protect his confidence?

- Honour and respect him.
- Listen to him.
- Never put him down in front of his friends or family.
- Particularly don't put him down in front of your children.

I remember when in 2015, my family was featured on a television show and the interviewers were speaking to one of my daughters. She highlighted that she had never heard myself and my husband argue, now she's almost thirty years old. I promise you, this does not mean that we have agreed on every single thing we have faced in the last thirty years. No. It simply shows that it is possible to discuss your concerns in a non-argumentative manner. And when you want to discuss especially touchy issues, you can do so in the privacy of your rooms (without the yelling).

Specifically, when you are dealing with the discipline and upbringing of your children, respect your husband's opinion. If he told them they cannot have something, don't give it to them behind his back. It may feel gratifying in the moment to be the "popular/friend" parent, but when your actions come to light, it will chip away at the joy and trust within your marriage relationship. If you disagree and believe they should have that item or that they don't need to be grounded for what they did, speak to him about it when they are not there.

Another core and foundational principle in being the wife of a happy marriage is submission and because it is such an in-depth and life changing matter, we have dedicated the entirety of Chapter Five to submission. For now, let us turn to some other matters that are going to be helpful to you as a wife.

Make Your Home A Safe Space

Make your home a loving environment that your husband wants to come back to at the end of each day. This includes your physical home (keeping it nice, neat and attractive) as much as is possible for you but more than physical cleanliness, having a welcoming home is about the atmosphere you cultivate.

When everyone in the house is moping about, sulking or yelling at each other, you have the power to change that atmosphere. Choose to let go of whatever the issue is, put a smile on your face and seek to make amends. If you just had a hard conversation, go out of your way to do something to lighten the air and show your husband that you are not sitting in the funk of it for the next week.

If you are upset, of course, there is a place to discuss those things that concern you, but here I speak particularly about the way some women hold on to grudges and a bad attitude for weeks out of one discussion. Don't allow the devil to steal the joy in your home. As soon as a thing is resolved, put a smile on your face, give your husband a kiss and move on like it was never there. When God forgives you, he doesn't hold you to it for one second after you have repented. He lets go and fully receives you, immediately.

> *Figure out what is most important to you. Highlight those things, but don't expect your husband to think and act exactly like you do.*

There is nothing more stressful than a nagging wife. When you've told your husband something once, give him time to act on it. Remember that there are some things that are never going to change. He just may never stop taking off his shoes in the middle of the living room everyday when he returns from work and leaving them there. So, what do you do? Clean up after him or nag and nag, get upset, equate that with him not loving or appreciating you and make it a huge negative focus until you break your marriage?

This is not excusing his bad habits but saying that your nagging him about them will not be the push he needs to change. Pray for him to change and then trust God to do the work. Some of us complain and nitpick on everything he does wrong or even those things he does half-right without noticing all that he does well for you. Before you complain about something, think - is this really a big deal? If it is not worth mentioning, don't mention it, just fix it. If you can see that he is genuinely trying to change or help in an area, allow him the room to grow and give suggestions when needed but don't make it the focal point of your conversations.

You can also figure out what is most important to you and highlight those things to him but don't expect him to begin to think and act exactly like you do.

Appreciate Him

I knew a man (Mr A.) during my stay in England, who would go shopping with his friend (Mr T.) for their respective wives. Mr T. would buy a gift worth £5.00 and Mr A. would look at it, scoff and buy a gift worth £50.00 for his own wife.

He was more wealthy and owned a car so he would be the one to drop off his friend at home before getting home himself. He noticed over and over that when he dropped off his friend, Mr T. would present his wife with the £5.00 gift and she would be so full of appreciation and gratefulness. Then he would continue home with his £50.00 gift smiling at the reception he expected to receive from his wife and almost always, she would simply look at it, take it from him and not even say thank you. This used to crush him over and over again.

You can learn a lesson from this. No matter what your husband gives you or does for you, learn to say thank you. Even if you already have three other pairs of red shoes in your closet (that he bought for you last year) and somehow he ends up getting you another pair of red shoes, say thank you and receive it! It means he likes you in red shoes! Give some of the extras away as a gift to someone else or a donation to charity or humorously show him your collection of red shoes and let him know the colors you need. Make it a joke and thank him for the gesture of love from your heart.

Plus from one wife to another, when you show appreciation for his acts of love and gifts, it encourages him to want to do more of the same which is also to your benefit.

Accept His Love

I spent all of Chapter Two reminding your husbands to show you acts of love through service, their words etc. When he begins to do these things, don't look at him like he is crazy. Make a conscious effort to receive his compliments and actions of love.

My daughter told me of a day when she had attended a poetry event with her husband and while there, they spoke of godly marriages and encouraged the men to see their wives with new eyes, to appreciate, encourage and love on them. Her husband had told her that was what stood out the most to him from the entire event. So when they got home, he began to lay on the compliments, not in cheesy way, but in a consistent, heartfelt manner. For the next few days, he reminded her of how much he loved and appreciated her and for some reason, she felt herself starting to get angrier and angrier. She shrugged off his compliments and didn't want to hear any more of it.

At a point, he asked her what the problem was, and she honestly replied that she didn't know why she was getting upset. She went into their bedroom to pray to God about it. In her time of prayer, God showed her that she was choosing to be offended because he had stopped displaying his affection to her with his words for a time and was picking it back up now that he had been reminded. Somehow, this equated to her heart focusing

> *Some of you may feel like your husband's display of love is too little too late, but that is only true if you make it so.*

more on the fact that he had stopped doing it for a time but in that place of prayer, the Lord reminded her to see the good in what was happening.

He said, "Your husband was reminded to show you extravagant love and decided to *do it*, and he's been doing it in a fresh way ever since! That's what matters here! Stop thinking about when or how long he stopped and start appreciating what is happening now. Remember that he is not perfect and can't be expected to remain consistent in every area at all times, and be willing to meet and receive his love as he learns and grows." She mentioned that even after she was corrected, it was still a choice to let go of the guilt she was holding over him and simply accept his display of love. But she chose to do it, left her room and time of prayer, went over to him and gave him a hug and a good kiss. She told him what she had been focusing on that had held back her delight, apologized for blowing off his renewed displays of love and told him she was willing to receive it. That encouraged him to continue and they both benefitted from that choice that she made.

Some of you may feel like your husband's display of love is too little too late, but that is only true if you make it that way. Remember that he is a human being and forgive him for forgetting to keep his love and appreciation of you active for however long he has forgotten it. Then choose to receive it today, and tomorrow and every other day he shows it. Smile, hug him, and respond in kind.

Be Willing To Apologize

When I was younger, I had such a hard time saying the word "sorry" that I would rather go without a meal than apologize to someone who would be at the dinner table. One day, my father called me aside and said "Tayo, if you can't say you're sorry at this age, you will have a very difficult time in marriage." That comment stuck to me and helped me to realize by the time I was getting married, that being able to apologize was a very important key to having a happy married life.

I believe this so strongly, that I don't just apologize when I'm wrong but sometimes, if I know it will bring a resolution, I apologize even if I am not the primary person at fault. I usually will find what part of that conflict I am responsible for and apologize for that thing even if it's a lesser "fault" than my husband's.

Some people will say this is stupid. But I would rather be happy than be proven right. Apologizing when I am wrong and giving room to my husband even when I'm right resolves so many issues immediately.

Ask yourself this question - do I want to be happy or do I want to be right? In many of those cases where I apologized and it wasn't my fault, I would go back to my husband when things weren't so tense anymore and let him know that I just apologized to him for something he did wrong and we would end up talking and laughing about it.

Many married couples are living in misery and by the time they have brought me into the picture, we find that their misery is being perpetuated by themselves. They refuse to forgive, forget or let go of the faults of the other person. And it ends up causing a corrosive relationship.

As a wife, you must understand that sometimes, just for the sake of preserving your marriage, home and peace, you need to apologize and step back.

So then, if you bring your gift to the altar and there remember that your brother has something against you, leave your gift there in front of the altar. First go and be reconciled to your brother and then come and present your gift.
Matthew 5:23-24

Finding Balance

A lot of times people ask me how I am able to balance it all. How I can be a wife (of a pastor which means a mother to many), an entrepreneur with three thriving businesses, a practicing lawyer, an administrator and director of two shelters, a mother of five daughters, an international speaker and itinerant preacher and still have my children and husband be able to genuinely thank God for my life and character. Most people would assume that a woman who is thriving in her career is suffering on the home front or vice versa but that is absolutely not true if you are able to learn from God how to balance it all. Also, if you do what God is calling you to do - nothing more and nothing less. But let's speak to those who are called into roles that do require a lot from them.

One of the biggest things the Lord taught me that has helped to balance these vastly different roles has been to have my priorities in the right place. That is why priorities is one of the very first issues I address in the Dealing With Conflicts section of this book. Knowing your priorities as a wife and for some of you, mother, is the absolute key to keeping a healthy life balance.

> *Knowing your priorities as a wife and for some of you, mother, is the absolute key to keeping a healthy life balance.*

This means recognizing that your husband needs your attention. Myself and my husband have had a solo vacation once every year for as many years as I can remember. It doesn't have to be extravagant or expensive. Take some time to separate yourselves from the noise and distractions, to look each other in the eyes without any interruptions and remember why you got married in the first place.

Outside of that, I am constantly talking to and texting my husband throughout the day. Even if we don't see each other until nighttime and sometimes late at night, he usually knows where I am, what I'm doing and how my day is going as it unfolds. Also, outside of specific deadlines and periods with much work to be done, I try to spend a few evenings in the week sitting and joking around with him and the children who are still living with us, watching TV and doing nothing productive!

As an international speaker and minister, I choose to submit to my husband by running every preaching and ministry invitation I receive by him. This is done for three reasons. One, it helps me to stay humble and grounded knowing that I am going with my husband's blessing and covering. Also, he sees my blind-spots and has permission to let me know when I am looking way too tired or have too many things happening at the time to take on something new. Thirdly, it ensures that he knows my travel schedule and it doesn't conflict with his. There are weekends he needs me by his side at events he is preaching at, or he plans on having a church program which is a priority for me as well, or he will be traveling soon after and it will be best for us to spend that weekend together because it will be the last in a few weeks.

This may seem unnecessary but it is the point of marriage, for him to be able to see that this decision won't be in my best interest and point it out to me in a loving way.

Cooking And Cleaning

Because I have such a busy schedule, many children and tons of guests coming by the house at any given moment, I cook in bulk. I take time on the weekends to prepare a few different soup dishes (big pots), some rice (jollof, fried rice etc) and maybe one other dish. Then I put most of it in the freezer and everyone can get what they need even when I'm not home. I personally consider it part of my duty to have food prepared for my husband and children as well as whatever they need for school (clothes etc).

At this stage in my life, most of my daughters still living with us can cook and clean which helps. If there's a week where they have too much on their plate and I do as well, I will usually pay a cook to make a bulk meal like I described above and we all can use that for the week.

Mothers Of Young Children

More than ever, your home has to be your priority when you have young children. You cannot sacrifice your husband and children on the altar of your career.

Before I migrated to Canada, I was a practicing lawyer in Nigeria for fifteen years. I came with five young children and back then, I knew that if I were to follow my legal career path at that time, I would not be able to give my children the priority they needed.

So, for the first eight years after we migrated to Canada, I changed my career and went to work in social services. It was less pay for hard work but worth it to me because I could be home when my children were leaving for school, then leave for work and be back when they returned.

I only decided to go back to my legal career after my fifth daughter had gotten enrolled in and started full-day school. Now I have finished all the bar exams, have been called to the Canadian Bar and run a successful legal practice. Most importantly, with my family intact.

Be aware of what season you are in, take time and focus on one thing at a time. Build where needed and be willing to make sacrifices for the sake of your marriage.

Work

If you want to build your home, have a thriving career, be in ministry or volunteer in your community in an active way, it will take hard work. Especially if you want to do these things in excellence. You will have to wake up earlier than your peers and you will go to bed later than them. You will need to learn how to manage your time effectively. You have to cut some things out of your life -

Useless chatter

You don't have the time to sit on the phone with friends who have no goals for their lives. I am serious. Look through your recent calls list and ask yourself, what are the active goals of the people I spend most of my time chatting with? Where are they going? Not where they say they are going, but where are their actions projecting for them?

Constant parties/events

Mrs. I promise you, If you try to be the social butterfly you were at the age of eighteen when you had no responsibilities, you will not reach all the places you desire to go. You cannot be at every party and life event for everyone on your rolodex. I can't tell you how many events and functions I have missed for the sake of focusing on what is most important to me. This doesn't always feel good, but is necessary. You cannot go to parties every weekend if you are trying to build a balanced life that impacts many people.

Frequent friend visitations

Hospitality is a quality that I greatly cherish and I personally have an "open door policy" which means anyone can drop by to see us whenever they choose. I do not have very frequent friend visitations. This is similar to the useless chatter/phone calls. I am talking to those wives who spend more time at their friends' homes or have friends over consistently. You don't have time for that. You chose to marry your husband for a reason. Because he was your favourite friend at the time. Spend the time with him that is necessary to ensure he remains your favourite friend!

You must manage your time wisely.

Overall, the largest part of getting balance in your life, and having good time management is learning the skill of saying NO. Learn to take ownership of your life, put your relationship with God first, your family second and then make decisions that push you towards your goals and not away from them.

But My House Must Be Spick and Span!

Sometimes your house is not going to be clean. *That's ok*. If you have children, be prepared for them to get engaged in a lot of activities in their community and at the church as they get older. This means they may no longer be able to assist you in taking care of the home like they did when they were younger. This is one of the reasons why it is valuable to have your husband give a helping hand (See Chapter Twelve, Chores And Expectations).

But guess what? You can also not expect to have a perfectly clean house while your children are toddlers and young. It doesn't mean you shouldn't try, but that they probably will be messing it up as you are cleaning it up and that's ok. Don't stress it and don't allow others to make you feel ashamed for having a home that looks like it's being lived in. Do what you can with the strength that you have and leave the rest for tomorrow, then when tomorrow comes, do what you can with the strength that you have.

There was a point in my life where I didn't have the time to have a perfectly clean home all the time. Both my husband and I did the best we could, but when it wasn't perfect we both understood and didn't allow that to become a stress factor in our lives. During that time, my friends would come over and actually comment that it didn't look neat and tidy, and I remember telling them that if it bothered them so much, they should help me clean it themselves. I was physically exhausted and my children couldn't help at that time because they were either too young or out changing the world doing some community activities (which I had encouraged them to do).

Am I telling you not to keep a clean house? No. I am saying don't kill yourself trying to impress other people.

Church Involvement as a Mother/Wife

Sometimes as women in the church, we allow ourselves to be pressured into thinking that we need to be at every single meeting that is called. If you yield to that pressure, you will be stressed, exhausted and won't give your family the attention they need because you are so busy building other people's families and helping them in the church.

I am not saying use your children as an excuse not to attend weekly church programming that will help you grow in your spiritual walk with God, but have your priorities right and manage your time well enough to balance both.

There are times you will not be able to attend the prayer meeting because you haven't cooked dinner. In those cases, stay home and *cook dinner*! There are times you will not be able to go to the bible study because you need to take your child to a program. First, try not to schedule your children's weekly programming for the same time you know you have a church meeting that will help you grow. But if there is a conflict in one week, there is no sin in taking your child to their program.

There are times even as a pastor's wife, I respectfully excuse myself because there is a pressing family need. There is nothing wrong with that.

> *As much as you are learning in the church about being a good mother or wife, you cannot put it into practice sitting in those pews.*

Moreover, some churches have a church service almost every single day of the week and then on top of that, they have phone prayer meetings as well almost everyday of the week. I do not want to be misunderstood, I believe in fellowshipping with the brethren. I believe in it so much that I have and continue to invest a large part of my time serving God within the context of the local church. I also believe in the power of prayer, and in seeing women participate wholeheartedly in their local church. But if your church demands every single day of your life, you need to use your head, think and think well. As much as you are learning in the church about being a good mother or wife, you cannot put it into practice sitting in those pews. You have to take it home and spend that time with your family.

The reality of many sincere Christian's lives is that the first place that suffers, the thing they usually have to give up to be a part of these programs is their family. When this happens, their family becomes a prayer point at the meetings they are attending. Yet it is mainly due to the neglect and lack of attention that it was given. Some people actually end up losing their families on the altar of the "church". This is not what God intended at all.

This matter is escalated when you are married to a husband that is not a Christian. Part of submission is acknowledging his viewpoint and using wisdom in balancing your church activities with his wishes. Remember that God is not limited to your church's four walls. He can meet with you at home. You don't need to follow such a husband into sin, but some of the requests he is making of you are not sinful, they're common sense. The bible says, get wisdom and with all your getting, get understanding.

I will say it again women, ensure you are fulfilling the obligations to your home before you run off to church. This has meant for me - hard work. I often come home from a full day of work, cook dinner and then prepare a sermon all within two hours, before going to a church meeting and serving until nighttime. Then to return home and prepare into the early morning for my next day's work and then wake up early in order to pray, wake up the children and head to work. Where there is a will, there is a way. If you want to be present at your church's functions, make sure you have taken care of your family first.

The Importance Of Prayer And Trusting God

As a wife, I believe that you are a primary intercessor for your family. Remember that your strength comes from the strength of your relationship with God. That is why your personal relationship with God should always be top priority. Remember that God's thoughts toward you are of peace and not evil. He is with you to see you through every situation.

For example, when you don't agree with your husband, negotiate, and if he still disagrees, don't make it an issue, make it a prayer point. Don't rant, scream or make a fuss. If it is God's will, He can speak to your husband or change his heart. If he doesn't, that means it is not necessary from His perspective and when you trust God's leadership, you are much more likely to trust your husband's leadership.

Physical Appearance

When you get married it is so important not to allow the things your husband loves about you to begin to fall apart. Things like your personal hygiene, hair, physical appearance and even your humour.

Many women don't realize that self care, personal appearance and personal cleanliness mean a lot to their husband's. You married him at a size eight and within a short time, you're pushing on size eighteen. Whether you like it or not, many marriages have been broken or very negatively impacted because of this.

You may say that is vanity, that if a man is to leave his wife because she has gained that much weight, he never loved her in the first place, but I don't believe that he did not love her before. I don't endorse that sort of response to even drastic weight gain, but I have to caution you to take your health and weight seriously. For better or worse doesn't mean you should actively allow it to become worse for him. Of course, looks aren't everything but they were a definite part of how he was first attracted to you. Your character, personality and temperament came after he saw you.

Most of us add weight almost automatically when we settle into marriage (many men do as well).

> *The goal here is not to be "skinny". The goal is to maintain a healthy weight.*

Having children also amplifies the weight gain for many women. Yet, keeping and continuing the weight gain usually comes from an indiscipline in eating, exercise and lifestyle choices (consistently drinking sugar filled drinks, stuffing our faces with pastries, all sort of carbohydrates and fried foods combined with a lack of physical activity).

Skinnier does not equate to more beautiful, so the goal here is not to be "skinny". The goal is to maintain a healthy weight. Many of us have a reckless abandonment about the matter of our health and have stopped caring or trying. That is what I am trying to address.

For many of you, you get angry and defensive if anything is remotely mentioned about weight gain or being big. Even if it didn't come up maliciously. If your husband can not tell you that you are gaining weight, who do you expect to tell you? Wouldn't you prefer that he helped you notice that you have started down that path before you realize it five sizes later? I promise you, no one is going to be looking at you as closely as he is, so don't bite his head off if he happens to say something to you about it.

Decide to do something about your health and weight. Even if you have tried before and feel like you weren't able to really get a hold of it then, don't give up! Keep on reading books, ask friends around you who are maintaining a healthy lifestyle. Some of you need to pray and break agreements you have made with gluttony. Repent to God for running to food when you are stressed instead of to Him. Deal with both the spiritual, mental and practical side of the issue. Make lifestyle choices that will help you live longer to enjoy your family and marriage. Get active.

If you are like me and can't keep up in group fitness classes, go for long walks with the hubby, take the stairs instead of the elevator, go swimming, buy an exercise machine or home gym (and actually use it). Go running with your friends. Hit the gym again and if you can't afford a gym membership, use YouTube videos to workout at home. Make an effort, I can assure you, you will feel more confident, look more attractive, be healthier and add years to your life.

Looking Good For Your Husband

Your physical appearance within the marriage is more than your weight, it's also about your presentation. This is something you can do really well no matter what your current weight is. Imagine this- you made an effort to make yourself attractive and appealing to him before you got married. Now, you wear ugly bras, underwear from years ago with holes in it, your hair is always a mess and your nails have chipped polish while you're at home.

But when you are going out, you style your hair nicely or put on a wig, get your nails done, put on a body shaper, your best underwear, some or lots of makeup, look great and show out. How do you think that makes your husband feel? Like you don't care about being attractive for him.

While other women are outside flaunting what they have in front of your husband, you are presenting yourself to him like an old maid while at home. No man wants that. No man wants his wife to become a slob. (Husbands, I will add here that no woman wants her husband to become a slob either!)

I already mentioned in that we normally take vacations each year. During our vacations, you can be sure that I bring good looking lingerie along and wear a different one each day. He is a Pastor to everyone else, but he is my only husband and I am his only wife.

Shake things up sister!

Get yourself some sexy lingerie. Bring that Valentine's day feel often through the year. You may not feel "in the mood" all the time but allow yourself to make things happen for him.

Keep in mind, your husband can have sex with you every day of the week and still feel emotionally rejected because he can see that you are just going through the motions. He longs to know that he is pleasing you and that you are sexually interested in him.

This partly explains the lure of sexual outlets like porn these days. The sexual images of provocative women around aren't only about their exposed (and airbrushed) body parts, but the most sexual thing about them is their availability. Their eyes and pose say to the men looking, "I want you, and I won't reject you!"

Read Solomon's description of a woman who tries to

entice a man into adultery:

She threw her arms around him and kissed him, boldly took his arm and said, "I've got all the makings for a feast — today I made my offerings, my vows are all paid, so now I've come to find you, hoping to catch sight of your face — and here you are!

I've spread fresh, clean sheets on my bed, colorful imported linens. My bed is aromatic with spices and exotic fragrances. Come, let's make love all night, spend the night in ecstatic lovemaking! My husband's not home; he's away on business, and he won't be back for a month.

Proverbs 7:13–20 (The Message)

No no, Mrs., your husband is yours and only yours for the taking. Rekindle the fire and let the fireworks begin.

Self Care

Self care is also more than watching your weight. It touches on your entire physical, emotional, mental and even financial well being. It is taking care of yourself holistically and bringing your best self to the table everyday by getting the rest and balance you need.

For example, getting enough sleep and doing those things you love like reading, biking or swimming. When you need to, take a vacation alone and refresh. It could be for just one weekend, in a hotel just outside of your city. Some of you are thinking, "I can't afford to do that". The truth is you can't afford not to. If you're tired and stressed beyond your capacity, you aren't helping anyone.

When you are concerned about something, pray about it. The bible says that you should not be worried or anxious about anything because neither of those things can actually change your situation.

Don't hold on to bitterness, grudges or hatred. It will affect your own health and has been scientifically proven to amplify many different diseases. The bible says, as much as it depends on you follow peace with all men.

Self Development

An important part of self-care that God revealed to me many years ago is having a strong plan for personal self-development. Wives, do not give up on your dreams! Always push to grow, change and expand your borders. Go back to school. Do a short course on a subject you enjoy.

Develop a business you love. Stop procrastinating about doing those things you know you were created for. Most of all, don't listen to all the "Debbie Downers and Naysayers" around you who always think that sitting down and doing nothing is safer than stepping out and making a difference. That option is also boring and wasteful!

I believe that with the wisdom of God, any woman is able to grow in her ability to impact to the world around her. It will do a lot for your psychological wellbeing as well as your social wellbeing. Growing mentally and being useful outside of your home will actually make you a happier, more fulfilled wife which will positively affect your own family in the long run.

Both you and your husband should sit together, share your dreams and cooperate in seeing them happen. Like Romans 12:10 says, preferring one another in love, pursue those dreams and support each other. Like my people say, take it "turn by turn".

On aircrafts, they normally announce that in the case of an emergency, you should put on your oxygen mask first, before you put it on your child. In the same way, you need a healthy you, in order to build a healthy home and make your marriage work.

Most importantly, remember that "physical beauty is not a substitute for a lack of discretion or discernment. Outward beauty without godly conduct has no lasting value."

–International House Of Prayer, Kansas City

Mentorship and Community Service

Community service and hospitality are a key part of your christian walk as well as your marital experience. It is really important to give back to society as well as to be hospitable. The bible is full of women who through their hospitality not only blessed their own homes but were blessed in the process.

A few examples are Dorcas, the woman who helped to sew coats and garments for so many people in her town and when she died, they refused to allow her to simply pass away. They sent two men to call Peter over and asked him to pray that she would be raised up from the dead. Can you imagine that? As small as Dorcas may have been, her effect was powerfully felt in her community.

Another form of community outreach is choosing to be a mentor to younger women. Make yourself available and be willing to be a trustworthy accountability and prayer partner to younger wives as well.

Likewise, teach the older women to be reverent in the way they live, not to be slanderers or addicted to much wine, but to teach what is good. 4 Then they can urge the younger women to love their husbands and children, 5 to be self-controlled and pure, to be busy at home, to be kind, and to be subject to their husbands, so that no one will malign the word of God.
Titus 2:3-5

This has a twofold impact. One, you are blessing to another woman, helping her to build a strong god-fearing home. Also, iron sharpens iron as you counsel the younger women, it will force you to review you own habits and practices and ensure that you are honouring God in all.

A word of caution - as blessed as it is to run a hospitable and open home, you do need to use wisdom. I have seen many homes broken by foolish decisions. For example, a wife allows an unmarried woman/friend to come and live in her home and it ends up breaking her marriage.

Be mindful of the company you keep. If your friends are flippant about their own marriage covenants, or interfering in other people's marriages, find new friends.

Charm is deceptive, and beauty does not last; but a woman who fears the LORD will be greatly praised.
Proverbs 31:30 (NASB)

Finally I will say this, you, Mrs., are not your husband. You were created differently and with a specific purpose in mind. You are a good treasure that God has given to your family and you are valuable beyond measure. Choose to see your value, celebrate your marriage and have fun!

5

The Power Of Submission

It is in willing submission rather than grudging capitulation that the woman in the church (whether married or single) and the wife in the home find their fulfillment."

—ELISABETH ELLIOT

I once counselled a young woman a few months before her wedding. I was talking to her about the importance of living a submissive life as a wife and she said point blank, "I don't think I can do this submission thing. It's not a part of me and I just don't want to."

I responded to her that in her case, getting married would be a terrible road to go down. "If you do not love this man or respect him enough to submit to him, you shouldn't be getting married to him at all."

No matter how educated, smart, unknown, popular,

poor or wealthy you are as a woman, submitting to your husband will both empower you and help you have a much happier marriage.

This topic is not a popular one in our day but it is necessary to discuss. I believe that the reason submission is not a favoured term, is because many people have the wrong thing in mind when they think of it. I am not referring to an oppressive choice to live under a dictatorship in your home. And it also does not mean putting up with an abusive relationship.

For some men, submission means that the woman is their doormat. It's a tyrannic type of leadership where the she has no say. That wife is not under submission, she is under oppression. If you are demanding submission from your wife, that is not loving leadership. Even Jesus Christ tells the church to follow Him but He allows us to make our own choices at the end of the day. He is looking for a loving choice on our part, not a forced obedience.

As a woman and mother of five women, I fight for women's rights in the course of my everyday work and in almost everything I do, but I don't agree with feminism in the way it is defined and acted out in our culture. I do not agree with the notion that because a woman is completely independent, she should do anything she wants, when she wants, how she wants without regard for any authority figure. Before you are an independent woman, you are a child of God and you have been bought by the blood of Jesus. When you chose to accept Christ, you chose to come under God's authority. When you chose to get married, you chose to come under your husband's leadership.

With that said, submission can actually be a joyful and

powerful thing if you embrace it by the grace of God. When you choose to submit not because it's a requirement but because you love the person you are submitting to.

What Is Submission?

To begin, I will share a quote from John Piper's article "Husbands Who Love Like Christ and the Wives Who Submit to Them".

"Submission does not mean putting the husband in the place of Christ. Verse 21 [of Ephesians 5] says you submit out of reverence for Christ. Submission does not mean that the husband's word is absolute. Only Christ's word is absolute. No wife should follow a husband into sin. You can't do that in reverence to Christ. Submission does not mean surrendering thought. It does not mean no input on decisions or no influence on her husband. It does not come from ignorance or incompetence. It comes from what is fitting and appropriate (Colossians 3:18) in God's created order.

Submission is an inclination of the will to say yes to the husband's leadership and a disposition of the spirit to support his initiatives. The reason I say it's a disposition and an inclination is that there will be times when the most submissive wife will hesitate at a husband's decision. It may look unwise to her. Suppose it's Noël and I. I am about to decide something foolish for the family. At that moment

Noël could express her submission something like this: "Johnny, I know you've thought a lot about this, and I love it when you take the initiative to plan for us and take the responsibility like this, but I really don't have peace about this decision and I think we need to talk about it some more. Could we? Maybe tonight sometime?"

The reason that is a kind of biblical submission is that

- Husbands, unlike Christ, are fallible and ought to admit it.
- Husbands ought to want their wives to be excited about the family decisions because Christ wants us to be excited about following his decisions and not just follow begrudgingly.
- The way Noël expressed her misgivings communicated clearly that she endorses my leadership and affirms me in my role as head."

Submission is having a heart that is willing to accept the man as the head and leader of the home. As your guide. For example, let's look at your marriage like a ship. In that ship, you and your husband may both have the gifting and understanding required to guide the ship. But the truth is that if both of you are at the helm of the ship, trying to steer and direct it at the same time, you are likely to pull that ship in different directions because you are two different people with different life experiences and perspectives. And also because of your differences as a man and a woman. In this scenario, if you both continue to fight over the wheel, that ship is going absolutely nowhere!

Loving headship and submission looks like the wife sharing her perspective in a kind, non-manipulative manner, the husband listening genuinely and using her input in his decision making. Then the wife letting go of the wheel and allowing him to make a decision for the family and then standing behind him in the decision that was made.

Now I would like to address reasons why it is important for your marriage, some of the challenges that you may be facing in submitting to your husband along with clear solutions for each reason.

Why Submit?

First, we submit to our husbands, because Jesus submitted to His Father's will. It is a form of sharing in the joys and sufferings of Christ.

Another major reason is that your husband's psyche thrives when he receives respect from his wife and submission is a sign of respect. Just like you desire affection from your him, he desires respect from you.

It doesn't feel good at times and that is because it goes against our sinful rebellious nature. That doesn't sound good to the ears but it's true. The difficulty in submission is not just seen in women's hearts but also in men because the bible also tells men to submit in the phrase "you all submitting to one another" (Ephesians 5:21). Also, we aren't just called to submit to our husbands but all Christians are called to submit to the authority that God has placed over our lives and every time submission to any authority is discussed, it is difficult for some to trust God's word and do it.

This is primarily because of the abuse of authority and leadership that have seen played out in human history. However, the failures of men do not exempt us from the commandments of God. He knew the frailty and weakness of those in authority over us and still asks us to submit.

Husbands, you are responsible for loving in such a way that submission is easier not because you are perfect but because the Mrs. can trust that even when she disagrees with the decision you are making, you are genuinely making that decision based on what you feel the Lord is saying, your love for her and the family and therefore she can trust the direction you are leading them in.

Symptoms Of An Unsubmissive Wife

ACTION POINTS

Mrs., take some time to quietly reflect on the following characteristics and search your heart and behaviour to see if this is in you.

I would like to make it clear that this section is not to be used against the Mrs. by the Mr. but is given as a tool for honest self-reflection. Some of you may be living as unsubmissive wives and not know what that looks like or think there is any issue with these actions. If the Mr. is reading this section, he should also examine himself because leadership and headship does not look like any of these actions being done toward your wife either.

- Putting down your husband (publicly or privately). Highlighting his mistakes and failures consistently. I'm not talking about the iron sharpening iron conversations that are part of your marriage which help build both of you up. I am talking about a condemnatory, complain-filled approach that highlights his faults over and over again. Especially if it is the highlighting of the negative consequences of a decision he has made. Not just pointing it out once for growth but in a nagging way.

- Being unwilling to listen to his counsel. Do you think your way is the safest and wisest option and fight for it almost every time?
- Talking over your husband. Are you exerting yourself over him in your conversations? Do you constantly interrupt him in the middle of his sentences?
- Always wanting to be in control. Do you have a "my way or the highway" approach, where no one is happy unless you "won" the argument or the decisions are made in your favor?
- Being manipulative. Do you use things like tears and undue pressure to get what you want? Nagging, excessive, consistent rehashing of issues, crying, denying him sex, outbursts of anger etc.
- Are you unwilling to go along with most directives or requests from your husband? Is something in you always challenging his authority even if when his requests are reasonable?

My Personal Self-Check

When I first got married, I thought I was a very submissive wife. I listened to my husband and respected him a lot. He is extremely smart and seven years older than me, so that alone gave me a strong basis for my respect.

Yet despite the respect I felt for him, I remember my cousin's wife would always tell me - "Tayo, you need to respect your husband" and I would wonder "What is she talking about? I already respect him".

Then one day she said, "You're always talking when he's speaking. You like to have the last word. It's like you think your ideas are better than his." My flesh did not like hearing those words but they were true and I needed to hear them if I was going to be a better wife.

I started to pay attention to my words. I decided that I wouldn't ever say anything derogatory to or about my husband. I also decided that I would do all that was in my power not to interrupt him mid-speech, even if I think just came up with a better idea. I learned to hold my tongue and hear him out completely when he's speaking.

It's thirty years later and I'm still not perfect in these areas and consistently have to be reminded by the Holy Spirit and a few around me when I do fall into the habit of speaking over him but I am conscious of this and have set my heart to submit to my husband in big and small matters.

If you found any of the points mentioned above in yourself or generally know that submission has not been an active priority for you, let us discuss how to submit. We will address the reasons why some women are hesitant to submit, then I will share some responses to these.

Why Is Submission Difficult?
Past Abuse Of Authority

Some of you wives, have been abused by people who were supposed to be in leadership over you. From absent fathers, to abusive family members, to church leaders who have manipulated and taken advantage of you in their decision making and other examples of imperfect leadership which has caused you to be wary of trusting a man to lead you completely.

Not Feeling Heard or Valued

Some of you may feel like you're not being heard within your marriage. You may feel like your opinion is not important or valued at all and like you have to nag, shout or take matters into your own hands if you want to have a say in your marriage.

Peer Pressure

Some of you have imbibed ungodly values being fed to you from media images of men having worthless leadership with women needing to take the helm. E.g. TV shows like "The Simpsons" depicting the man in the home as a good-for-nothing couch potato who does nothing but eat and get fat, who cannot keep the family organized. Shows that portray the woman as the only sensible leader in the home.

Some of you are being brainwashed by the opinions of your friends who tell you that submission is oppressive and stupid. And I'm not talking about unbelieving friends but even friends who go to church and profess to be Christian but refuse to live what the bible actually says. Friends who are not enjoying their marriages themselves but present a face of "empowerment" and the "perfect couple" at church on Sunday mornings yet go to bed angry, depressed and discouraged within their own marriages because they haven't keyed into God's way of doing marriage.

These friends always seem to have the most to say in giving you ungodly input on how to handle your marriage specifically when it touches on you needing to submit to your husband because after all "if it was them, they would NEVER go along with a decision like that", or they "cannot take nonsense from any man" etc.

The worst examples of this are those of you who are seeking advice from your unmarried or unsaved friends who are unable to encourage you in how to manage this in a godly, practical way.

Our Rebellious Sinful Nature

Finally a large part of why it is difficult for almost all of us to submit to our husbands is because of our sinful nature. It is a part of the curse that was placed on Eve. See when God cursed Eve, He said that her "desire" would be for her husband but he would rule over her. Here, I would like to defer to a quote from John Piper who expounded powerfully on this verse in an article on DesiringGod.org called "Manhood and Womanhood: Conflict and Confusion After the Fall"

> "Let's look at Genesis 3:16. Adam and Eve have both sinned against God. They have distrusted his goodness and turned away from him to depend on their own wisdom for how to be happy. So they rejected his word and they ate the fruit of the tree of the knowledge of good and evil. God calls them to account and now describes to them what the curse will be on human life because of sin. In Genesis 3:16 God says to the woman, "I will greatly

multiply your pain in childbearing; in pain you shall bring forth children, and your desire shall be for your husband, and he shall rule over you."...

So what is really described in the curse of Genesis 3:16 is the ugly conflict between the male and female that has marked so much of human history. Maleness as God created it has been depraved and corrupted by sin. Femaleness as God created it has been depraved and corrupted by sin. The essence of sin is self-reliance and self-exaltation. First in rebellion against God, and then in exploitation of each other."

It is this corrupt nature resulting from the curse placed on Eve that leads to our innate rebellion to the concept of submitting to our husbands.

All the reasons listed here are not worth you missing out on the joys that God has set aside for you in submission. They are genuine challenges that you need to acknowledge and deal with from the roots but they are not excuses to shy away from it. Unlike the woman I referred to in the beginning of this section, you are already married and it is too late for you to say "It's just not for me". Remember that there is no cookie-cutter solution as no two marriages are the same and no two husbands are the same.

Submission Solutions
Past Abuse Of Authority

In many of the examples I gave about this, it is not your husband who has abused the position of leadership over you and you need to forgive those people who have done this. The bitterness and resentment you may have been holding towards those people can be a part of what is currently hampering your ability to trust and submit to your husband at this time. So let them go. Forgive those people and trust God to lead your husband as he leads you.

> *Your husband needs you to trust him in order to show you a different style of leadership than what you've previously experienced.*

If your husband has made decisions that have hurt you in the past as well, choose to forgive him and begin a journey of rebuilding trust once again. Pray and ask God to give him the wisdom he needs to make good choices on behalf of your family.

Your husband needs you to trust him in order to show you a different style of leadership than what you've previously experienced. Remember that he isn't perfect and submission doesn't equal blind obedience. You are able to discuss together, and trust that he can make the final decision afterward.

Not Feeling Heard or Valued

If you feel your husband is not listening to you or that you aren't being given an opportunity to give input in decisions that affect the family. Or you feel your husband has taken this leadership and headship thing to the head and isn't giving you any room or flexibility in his form of leadership, I would counsel you to start with prayer.

Pray for him to learn what loving leadership looks like.

After you have prayed genuinely for him and forgiven him for any offense you may feel, speak with him and tell him how you feel. Remember you are both on the same team and your goal is to have a marriage filled with harmony.

You can say something like "when you consistently make decisions without considering or asking for my input, I feel ignored and excluded from the process. I'd like us to talk more about things before you go ahead and make a decision and I'd like to feel like you're listening to me."

Ensure that your approach is not done in an accusatory or judgmental manner so that the conversation doesn't escalate into something you did not intend. Take responsibility for moments when you have not previously been willing to submit so that he sees that you are not just highlighting his faults but willing to put yourself on blast as well. Finally, be willing to compromise and meet halfway.

Peer Pressure

I normally say this to couples that I counsel before they get married, don't take family decisions to your friends for their input. If you genuinely need help and counsel in dealing with conflicts within your marriage, take those concerns to a trusted spiritual leader who is able to objectively help you to find a godly solution. Your family's struggles should not be the subject of tea-time conversation with your friends. Not even if they ask!

Also, here is a huge and foundational rule of thumb to go by in selecting your friends after being married. If you have any friends who counsel you in a way that brings division and disunity to you and your husband, you better run away from them! Remember that you are the one sleeping beside that man everyday, not them.

They may have the best ideas for their own marriages but it isn't necessarily what is needed in yours. Also, if their counsel leads to a separation or divorce, these friends will not drop their lives to come and live with you. No! They would sympathize with you about the broken marriage and after one month, go back to their own thing while you are left picking up the pieces for the rest of your life.

All I am saying is, do not listen to those people who are counseling you against submitting to your husband, it is simply not godly counsel.

Our Rebellious Sinful Nature

Bringing our rebellious sinful nature under submission to God's word and leadership is a daily battle that has to be fought whether we like it or not. It is amazing because when we are willing to live God's word, we are freer in our relationship with Him. It produces great fruits of love, joy, peace and more in our own hearts and families.

How do we overcome our inner desire to be unsubmissive? Read the Bible and what it has to say to wives about submission. Also read other parts of the bible that speak on humility, read Matthew 5-7 (the sermon on the mount) and generally ask God to help you be more like Jesus Christ.

What If I Don't Agree With Him?!

I'll start by saying this - submission isn't submission if you agree with your husband. You don't need to "submit" to someone else's directives if you were already going in that direction yourself. Submission comes into play when you do not agree completely with the decision that is being made. *That* is your opportunity! Otherwise, you are already having your way. I hope you understand this.

Now, this isn't to say that it is an easy task. In fact for some of you it may feel extremely difficult. But it really shouldn't be if it's coming from the right pace. If it stems from a genuine desire to follow God's directive and from a place of loving and respecting your husband.

The How Of Submission

- Remember you are accountable to God, not your husband.
- Pray for the grace to obey His word and be a submissive wife.
- Choose to no longer speak unkindly to or about your husband (publicly or privately).
- When he makes mistakes (which he will), encourage him to do better. Pray for him and let him know you are in his corner. Highlight blind spots he may have not seen in a loving and respectful way.
- Listen to his counsel and go along with it. Accept that your way isn't the best option for every situation. In fact, even if it is an "ok" or better alternative in your opinion, choose his way on purpose!
- Stop talking over your husband. Yes! It's as simple as that. If you tend to interrupt him all the time, allow him to finish his thoughts and sentences.
- Relinquish control of your family. Decide to trust your husband as the leader of your home. In your heart,

mind and maybe even verbally, give him back the reins. Be willing to follow where he feels God is leading.

- Fight against manipulation. When you have genuine concerns, don't beat around the bush and hide them. Be clear in your communication. When you bring these concerns to the table, choose to no longer use tears, blackmail, bribery and other forms of manipulation. Give him your thoughts and counsel and let him do whatever he wants with it. Trust him to make the right decision without your coercion.

Lastly, in order to submit realize that it will add great strength to your marriage. When you allow your husband to function in his God-given role, you will both thrive. It really becomes a win-win situation where your submission causes him to love you more and his love causes you to be more willing to submit. It's a beautiful cycle which someone has to kick off, let it be you!

Consequences of Not Submitting

A friend (Mrs V.) once told me of a much younger newly-married lady who was trying to make a huge decision about schooling and child care that would greatly affect her life and marriage. Her opinion on what to do was very different from what her husband thought and when she discussed the matter with a group of friends (Mrs V. included), most of her younger friends counselled her to do exactly what she wanted to do despite the concerns and disagreement of her husband. They touted that it was "her life to live" and she needed to assert her independence and do what is best for her regardless of it's effect on her marriage or children. "After all, we live in Canada, you're not a slave in your own home".

Mrs V. who had been in a long-term fruitful and joyful marriage relationship counselled her to take into serious consideration what her husband was saying and probably go along with it as whatever decision she made would affect their marriage relationship and family for years.

Mrs V. pointed out to me that the majority of the women who were counseling this woman in that manner were separated or divorced professionals who were living an "independent" life at the expense of their marriage relationships. (This is not to say that all divorced or separated professionals are so because of this mindset. It was simply the case in this situation).

In this example, her friend went ahead with their advice and for the next few years, continued to meet with Mrs V. in particular, asking her how to handle the many challenges that resulted from that decision. At that point this young lady could not reverse her decision or automatically restore the joy in her marriage. However, her commitment to begin to walk in unity with her husband and submission to him at that point helped to begin the restoration process.

This is one example of many that can be shared of the consequences of trying to skip out on submission. Some of you are currently feeling the tension that comes from having to fight over the wheel of your "marriage ship" every single day. You feel like you are always arguing about absolutely every little thing that comes up. Each decision regarding childcare, finances, sex and other marriage related matters seem to give the final blow that can crush your friendship. And this can be because you have not yet begun to submit to your husband's leadership on these matters.

Have You Previously Been Unsubmissive?

First repent to God for not leaning on His wisdom during your role as a wife. Practically, I would not suggest that you go to your husband and tell him verbally that you are henceforth committing to be a submissive wife. As this can become a temptation for him to nitpick at your actions when you slip up.

Make a mental note of it, write it down in a journal and if you feel you can trust this to your husband, let him know as well. Ask him to be patient in helping you transition into this. Understand that it is not a journey of one day but many years. Just as our sinful nature is subdued daily and we are made holy in a long-term process of sanctification, your desire to "rule over" your husband has to go through that process.

Finally

It's interesting that a lot of women find it easy to submit to other people's husbands. They will readily submit to their pastor and elders in the church, their husband's friends, their fathers etc. but marriage is the place where there is the highest resistance. The one place where it offers you the highest benefit and payback.

I would like to say to you Mrs., that submission is not weakness but your greatest source and display of strength in this marriage. So do it and enjoy its fruit!

6

Our Children, Our Joy

Live so that when your children think of fairness, caring, and integrity, they think of you.

—H. JACKSON BROWN, JR.

Some years ago, a Globe and Mail article stated that "disagreements about money, sex, children and housework have long been chafing points in modern marriages. But now that parenting has become a mass obsession, clashes over how to raise kids are enough to tip shaky relationships over the edge." [1]

In this chapter we talk about how to ensure your children do not become that negative tipping point for your marriage. We discuss how to raise them up so that they have a good foundation for the path God has for their lives.

Right now, our culture bullies many parents to back off from taking an active role in their developmental years and in sharing with them the values they need to learn and live by. But there are many portions of scripture that speak explicitly to parents about how God expects us to actively participate in the training and raising up of our children.

Your Children Need You

We currently live in an era of increasing illicit drugs that are being targeted at our children and youth. Where our children are being taught in schools that marriage does not have to be between one man and one woman. Children are being exposed to pornographic material as early as grade school under the guise of sex education and through active online campaigns directed at children. They are being told that sex outside of marriage is totally fine as long as it is done with a condom.

And at the same time, parents are totally abdicate the responsibility to teach their children about sexual matters in a godly and safe form. Always thinking it is too early to have "those conversations" and not acknowledging that those conversations are already being had in their playgrounds at school and on social media all around them.

As if these are not enough reasons to be concerned about the way our children are being raised, we are also seeing a dramatic increase in mental illnesses including depression and suicide ideation among youth. Peer pressure and bullying has always existed but with the rise of social media and the internet, the children who used to be bullied only in school now carry those comments and harassment everywhere they go. It cannot be taken lightly as it has become an issue of life and death for many children.

Interestingly, many people have no idea of how close their children have been to committing suicide. It is an uncomfortable conversation but one that we need to have. A quote I saw recently said "It's hard to live with teenagers, but it's harder to live without them".

Your children have a lot of battles they are fighting. What they need are parents who will fight in their corner through prayer and a commitment to godly parenting, not parents who will cause more stress and harm.

Training Up Your Children

Train up a child in the way he should go: and when he is old, he will not depart from it.
Proverbs 22:6

This passage of scripture is one of the most commonly quoted yet many parents are unwilling to take this responsibility head on. Too many parents are waiting for the church, the government, school systems and youth leaders to help mold their children into productive members of the society.

You have to remember that after loving your wife or respecting your husband, this is the next most important directive for those who have children. Most children develop their personality within the first five to seven years of their lives (though it will adapt and evolve throughout their lifetime) and what you sow into your child in these formative years will produce fruit - good or bad.

It is not enough to provide food, shelter and other basic needs for your children, you want to make it a priority to invest in your child socially, academically, financially, emotionally and spiritually.

Training takes time and effort. It means spending focused time with your children at some point in the day. You will need God's help to be a reflection of His love, grace and mercy to your children, I can promise you, it does not come naturally to anyone. It takes wisdom and understanding to know when to be firm and when to allow them to make their own mistakes.

And even with all your investing and training, you cannot control the path your child will take in life. But let me make one thing clear. If you neglect this responsibility in the name of busyness, work, entertainment or simple apathy, the world will train up your child. And that will not have a good outcome unless God intervenes later on in their lives.

YOUR ROLE AS A PARENT
You Are To Provide

One of your primary responsibilities is to provide for your children. This is not always an easy task depending on the family structure, income and environment where you live. However, you as parents are expected to provide food, shelter, clothing, healthcare and education for your children. There have been seasons where I have had to work three jobs in order to support our children in this way. Despite the fact that my husband makes provision for his family a priority, in that season I also had to step up to the plate and pitch in. As a parent, do what you can so that they have what they need. Ask for help if you need it. Don't allow pride to cause your children to suffer.

Remember this God is the ultimate provider for your family. So even in seasons of lack, you are able to bring your needs before God as a family, allow them to see you pray and see God answer your prayers.

Invest For Your Children

Another practical way you should provide for your children is to invest for them. You can do this in two ways. One, you should put money away in an investment for your children when you pass away. You can also invest in funds towards things like their education.

Many parents believe that money is so scarce it's impossible to invest for their children. I used to take my five daughters out to KFC every Tuesday for "Toonie Tuesdays" back when it actually cost a toonie (a Canadian two dollar coin). And one day it hit me that I could be investing the money I spent every Tuesday in their bank accounts. So we replaced KFC toonie tuesday with another activity and I started to put a meager $20/month into each of their accounts.

By the time I checked their accounts a few years later, I was shocked at how much I had accumulated for them. Investing in your children is a choice. Prioritize what really matters. Is having the latest tech item more valuable than making post-secondary education that much more accessible to them? No.

A good man leaveth an inheritance to his children's children...
Proverbs 13:22

Get Them Involved In The Community

Ignorance is not bliss, there are many programs that are beneficial for your child to be involved in if you take the time to research and help them get connected. Attend their parent teacher meetings and follow up on their academic progress. While creating your monthly family budget, allow for activities that will help them engage socially.

These programs or activities do not have to be cost intensive but you do need to make it accessible to your children by being willing to pick them up/drop them off. Encourage them to get outside and get involved in their community even if they don't feel like doing it. Get them plugged in to your church's youth programming (though that isn't to be their primary source of spiritual growth, you are). All of this helps them develop commitment and builds mentor networks and friendships that will serve them greatly later on in life.

Many of my children who actively participated in these sort of community activities ended up benefitting greatly in the form of scholarships and better job opportunities.

Have Fun and Moderation

Have fun with them, take them out and give them gifts. Remember in my Toonie Tuesday example, I didn't just stop our Tuesday outings all together, I replaced it with another family activity. Fun doesn't have to be costly. It is more valuable in the long-term to invest in their future than to squander money trying to impress them or your friends.

Also providing for your children does not mean giving them everything they ask for or expensive things. Parents who do that are not preparing their children for the reality of living life as an adult. You cannot have everything you want without doing anything to earn it. There are many parents who are trying to buy their children's love and impress their peers by getting unnecessary gifts and countless trinkets for their children. This creates an attitude of entitlement that does more harm than good.

As you provide for your children, you want to teach them about financial responsibility, frugality and the way to live in order for them to be able to build wealth themselves. Don't make them believe the lie that the person with the most "stuff" is the most well off. If you currently believe that yourself and are working to get more "stuff", read books like "The Millionaire Next Door" by Thomas J. Stanley so that you know enough about the basics of money to teach them properly how to manage it.

This balance of knowing when to get that item and when to say no is going to be a prayer journey for you. Ask Holy Spirit to let you know when it is a trinket to you but would be very encouraging for your child and when to stand your ground.

You Are A Caretaker

Though they may not agree, your time is much more valuable to your children than any amount of money you can give to them. Your children need you to spend focused time with them. Sitting down together watching shows on television whenever you get time with them does not help you get to know them.

You are to teach them more values than you give them valuables. Your presence over presents. So many children are starving for love and attention from their parents, who misguidedly spend all their time working to show their children love, but have missed the greater opportunity before them.

Get to know your children individually. I often hear parents say about their 'delinquent' or more appropriately put miserable and frustrated child – "I gave her everything! She is so ungrateful. What a waste of my resources. *What more does she want from me?!'*

> *Your child wants you, your attention, your time, your advice, your help, they want to see you at that important competition, even when they tell you not to show up*

I can answer that question for you that child wants you, your attention, your time, your advice, your help, they want to see you at that important competition, even when they tell you not to show up - they want you to ask if they'd like you to attend, be turned down and ask how it went afterwards. Not just to boost your ego but to boost their confidence and have someone to rejoice with when they win and a shoulder to cry on when they lose, both in their games at school and in the game of life.

How many of us have gone looking for love in the worst places and come out hurt and broken? We cannot prevent our children from making some wrong choices but we can let them know they are loved, accepted, and highly valued.

If you don't know what you would do in focused time with your children, Google it. You'll find more ideas than you need to fill an entire year with activities for yourself and your child(ren).

You are An Example And Mentor

Be imitators of me, just as I also am of Christ.
1 Cor 11:1

One thing that I have seen my children greatly value has been times when myself and my husband have chosen to invest wisdom in them and taken time to advise them. When they were younger, I am pretty sure they hated being woken up earlier than necessary for the school start time. But we would wake them up, share scripture with them and then discuss what that meant for our lives. There were other times where we would wake them up and share advice and encouragement for their lives.

We shared stories of biblical and twenty-first century heroes who overcame great odds and made a difference in the world and instilled in them the truth that they can do much more than what others may see. We taught them values like courage, integrity, discipline, hard work and the list goes on. But one thing we knew was that nothing we could tell them would make a bigger effect than the example that we lived for them.

When our family moved to Canada, myself and my husband were faced with a huge challenge in our careers. I was a practicing lawyer of fifteen years who was told my qualifications and experience from Nigeria did not cut it for the Canadian Bar. My husband was a working chemical engineer who was also informed that he would not be able to continue to work as a professional engineer unless he went through a full process of accreditation as well.

This was a serious obstacle to us and at the point of moving here, bills weren't going to wait until we had fully assimilated to begin to pile up. So I got three jobs and eventually settled into one of them.

Myself and my husband then both decided to do the new accreditation exams required for our careers and when we explained what we were doing to our children, we let them know that if we could go back to studying at the age we were at that time, they are able to improve themselves and do whatever is required of them to succeed in life.

I remember when my husband was writing his Professional Engineer of Ontario exam, he called the children together and told them that it had been twenty years since he last sat for an exam, then he went ahead to ace that process. Our teaching about academic excellence and not letting outside circumstances stop you from achieving your goals, was not as important to them as our example. This time and in many other situations, they saw us choose the value systems we taught them in our own lives and we believe this is one of the topmost practices that has produced the same values in their lives.

Your children want you to lead by showing them a good example of what a young man should be and example of what a young woman should be. Before they want a friend, they need a first responder. That child, that young man or woman is crying out for attention. They are not as strong and independent as they may present themselves to be, or we sometimes think they are.

The opposite of this is also true. When we teach our children godly value systems, or we go to church and shout "Amen! Hallelujah!" to sermons about love and kindness but live in an opposite manner at home, it is a glaring contradiction to your children that they cannot ignore.

There are way too many children that witness their parents abuse one another, receive abuse from their parents and those same parents put on their suits and dresses on Sunday to go and praise God together with the children. What example does that show to them?

God is not mocked and what is done in the home matters greatly to Him. It is not enough to pretend to be a perfect Christian family on the outside because they are the ones who are following your lead.

For example, if you smoke and drink alcohol, telling your children it's a bad habit that will destroy their lives is not enough, begin the journey to quit.

If you see character traits in yourself that you do not want replicated in your children or you do not want to affect your children negatively, pray for God to change you and take active steps of accountability with your spouse or a trusted leader in Christ to begin to change.

Children In Abusive Homes

One of the best examples you can show your children is honouring your marriage, your spouse and putting each other above yourselves. Children who are exposed to abuse are usually afraid and apprehensive. They are always on guard, watching and waiting for the next event to occur. They never know what will trigger the abuse, and therefore, they never feel safe. They are always worried for themselves, their mother/father who goes through the abuse as well, and their siblings. It can lead to feelings of worthlessness and powerlessness.

Many children who grow up with abuse are expected to keep it within the family, they are warned not to tell anyone, sometimes not even talking to their siblings about the abuse. Children from abusive homes can look fine to the outside world, but inside they are in agony. Their families are typically in a turmoil and highly dysfunctional. They may blame themselves for the abuse thinking if they had not done or said a particular thing, the abuse would not have occurred. They may also become angry at other family members for doing things to trigger the abuse. They may feel rage, embarrassment, and humiliation.

Abused children feel lonely and defenseless. They are starved for attention, affection and approval. Mom is so focused on surviving she is often not present for her children. Dad is so consumed with controlling everyone; he has no time for his children. These children become physically, emotionally and psychologically neglected.

Some homes do not have the adult being abused, only the children. If you know that your child is having to deal with an abusive situation, you are their caregiver. Get them out of there today! They need someone that will fight in their corner. That will speak up for them.

There are too many "Christians" who are causing great damage and offense to their children because of physical, emotional, verbal and even sexual abuse. The bible says that if you offend one of these little ones, it is better that a millstone is cast around your neck and you are thrown into the sea. God does not take the abuse of His children lightly.

You Are Their Peacemaker

Blessed are the peacemakers: for they shall be called the children of God.
Matthew 5:9

While your family may encounter many crises in life, don't allow your home to become a crisis. Learn how to walk in God's peace and demonstrate that to your children. Instead of becoming bitter, angry and a danger to be around when things are not going well, begin to ask God to show you how to live with that peace that passes understanding.

Some of you have grown up in homes where yelling at each other was the norm. Don't pass that "norm" on to your children. Allow them to grow up better than you did. When you get into disagreements with your spouse, honour one another, and go somewhere private to have those hard discussions.

A Confidant

It may sound idealistic but it is possible. Build a relationship with each of your children. Listen to them, hear their point of view until they are finished speaking and don't let them feel alienated.

Children, especially teenagers, are weird and hard to understand sometimes. I still do not understand my teenagers and I'm on the fifth one. I don't know...

- How can anyone study for an exam listening to music?
- How on earth can a child sleep till 2pm in the afternoon?
- How can anyone can step over a pile of garbage and not see it until I point it out… every time?!

Although I have to say that one day while I corrected one of my daughters for the 800th time for skipping piles of dirt when she had swept up, we realized that she was consistently not seeing the dirt because she actually needed glasses! So sometimes they have good reason. But most times they don't.

Even then, try to listen to them and understand where they are coming from. Just listening tells them that you value their input, opinion and that they matter. Notice the small positive things they do and don't only speak to them when it is time for correction. Even when you are correcting them, tell them something good about what they are doing and then show them where they need to improve or what they need to change. Give them credit as often as possible and take the time to celebrate their accomplishments.

> *Just listening to your child tells them that you value their input, opinion and that they matter.*

Promote trust in your relationship with them. When you are listening, have compassion and don't be judgmental. For goodness sake don't repeat what they have told you in confidence to someone else or use it against them in an argument. That will break all the trust you have built with them.

Give Clear Guidelines

Your child needs boundaries in order to grow up as a healthy productive member of society. You want to promote their creativity and leave them free to explore, but you have to remember that you are responsible for them until they are old enough to make their own decisions. Too many new parents are leaving the child to set the rules of the home and that is not the way anyone has ever been "trained". If our mandate was to train up our children, we cannot leave that training up to them.

Handling Mistakes

No child is perfect and though we want the best for our children, there will come a time when they make a mistake, big or small. The way you treat your child in these times will be one of the biggest impressions for them on what love looks like.

You cannot bring up their mistake over and over when you get into a disagreement with them. God does not do that to you and it is extremely unfair to do that to them. My own children are not perfect and have made their fair share of mistakes as well and those have been some of my hardest times in parenting. But I have always maintained that you cannot throw out the baby with the bath water. You cannot afford to burn that bridge with your child completely because of repeated mistakes. If you kick them out of the house for what they did, how do you expect them to stop?

When your child makes a mistake, first of all remember that you once were young and made your own fair share of mistakes. Prayerfully ask God how to handle the situation. Discipline them appropriately but also let them know that they are forgiven and will not be held to that mistake for the rest of their life.

Fathers, do not exasperate your children, so they will not become discouraged.

Ephesians 6:4

As you train up your child look out for the following ways you may be exasperating them or frustrating the destiny that God has for them.

Curses And Foul Language

Be careful what you speak over your children as your words have great authority. My husband shares the story often of his father's words. When he was a young boy, he was always in fights. Every single time his dad would come to get him from another fight, he would drag him back home and declare blessings over him even though it was in a rough tone. He would say things like "It will be well with you!", "You are a blessed child!", 'You are going to succeed!', 'God will turn your life around!'. I truly believe that my husband is now enjoying the fruit of God's blessing his father spoke over his life in those moments.

When your child does something wrong or fails at school are you quick to say things like "you're so dumb?!", "When will you ever get anything right?", "I can't believe I gave birth to you", "why can't you be more like your sister?" These words can kill your child. If you normally speak such curses and destructive language over any of your children, repent before God, break off the curses that you have spoken or agreed with and declare God's truth over them!

In fact, when other people speak curses like these over my children, I speak the truth and break the curse over them. A teacher once told one of my daughters that she would never get into college because at that time she was failing most of her classes. I told her that she would not only get through high school with good marks but she would get into University, not just college. And she did. She had to work hard for it and another teacher helped to encourage her later on in her time in high school, but how would she have been able to keep on trying if her parents agreed with the discouraging report from her teacher?

Don't Try To Live Through Your Children

Ensure that the goals you are encouraging them to achieve are their own and not the things you think would be great in your high school reunion report of how your children are doing. You cannot choose who your children will marry for them. Neither can you choose their career. They are the ones who will live with the choices they make and if you impose your will on them, it will lead to resentment and bitterness in the long run.

When they are facing tough academic decisions, don't impose your own way on them, help them to figure out what they excel at and encourage them in the path they choose. When they are old enough to begin to make decisions for themselves, trust that you have given them the proper foundation for those decisions. If you really do not agree with something they want to do, give them advice, pray for them but leave them to make that decision.

No Battle Lines

Trying to raise your children together can create stress for both of you because you both want the best for them but your views on "how to get there" tends to be different. Each of you may have a very specific idea of what your child should be taught and changing that ever so slightly can result in you no longer having a united front. But when raising your children, you have to start from the perspective that you are all on the same team. Yourself, your spouse, as well as your children. It is not me vs you or us vs them. Once battle lines are drawn in the house, the house becomes a battle front. If you already have that sort of a mentality in your home, it will take a conscious effort to break it down.

It is exceptionally important that you both discuss how you would like your children to be raised and agree on the values that need to be instilled in them. Children are a lot smarter than you think, at an early age they learn the skill of playing one parent against the other. They will ask one parent for something and when dad says no, they will go to mum and mum, oblivious to what has transpired says yes. If you do not notice this at an early stage, you can begin to argue over what looks like "an attack on your leadership" when it was simply ignorance of what you had said beforehand. In this case, you would both have to let your child know that once mummy says no, that's the answer and they cannot go back and forth.

DEALING WITH DISCIPLINE

Some parents run away from disciplining their children completely because they do not know how to do it in a loving and effective way. But the consequences of ignoring this parental duty will have a serious effect on the ability of that child to be a responsible, positively contributing member of society for many years to come. If you are unwilling to discipline your child at home, life will discipline them for you. This unwillingness to properly discipline your child may also have an effect on their eternal destiny.

You both grew up under different modes and methods of discipline. Some under a heavy hand and others had no source of correction or discipline and were left alone to figure out right from wrong. It is important for you to find a healthy balance for your children.

The most important thing to understand is that discipline is not about what makes you feel good or "in control", it is about what will most positively impact your children and help them understand right from wrong.

One of you is probably a bit "harder" on the discipline scale than the other and this could even switch between you on specific issues. When you disagree over things like how to discipline them, the time your teenagers should come home in the evening or when they should do their chores, do not show your disagreement in front of your children. Your children play the game "divide and conquer" really well and don't need extra help from you.

It may seem like a trivial thing but I remember a couple who lost their marriage over whose instructions and chores for the children were more important. Dad asked his son to do something, unknowingly, mum asked the son to do something different at the same time.

When dad found out, he was upset. A heated argument ensued as to whose chore was more important, dad pushed mum, one of the children called the police. Dad was arrested and charged and that was the end of their marriage. How simple would it have been for either of them to let go and give in to the other person?

Be Motivated By Love

It is hard to give godly counsel motivated by love if you have made the issue an argument or a personal challenge. Make sure they know that you love them. The advice you give and the correction you dish out has to be congruent with a consistent display of kindness, care and love. Otherwise, you become a clanging cymbal and a distant dictator. As you address the challenges that arise with the different stages of their lives, start here. I am not saying that you cannot be firm, in fact, they need you to set boundaries while learn how to make their own decisions.

Do Not Discipline A Child In Anger

When you discipline a child while angry, your discipline becomes disproportionate to the situation being handled. If you know you are very angry about what has taken place, give yourself time to cool off before you respond with an appropriate correction.

Help them Understand

Let them know why they are receiving that correction. Tell them what they were supposed to do not just what they did wrong. While growing up, at times I would be punished for doing something and have no idea what exactly I did wrong. What benefit is that to your child? How are they supposed to learn from that experience?

Don't Nag

Nagging is not discipline, it is just as irritating and annoying to your children as it is to you. Talk about the issue and leave it there. Do not go back to it every single day. No one wants to be woken up by someone yelling at them. Stop doing it. It does not enforce your viewpoint in a good way, it only hardens them toward what you're saying. Pick your moments, pick your battles.

Start Early

Many parents do not realize that a child forms their character by the time they are five years of age. They want to spoil them rotten until they are twelve and suddenly start to instill discipline at age thirteen. It does not work that way. For many parents it is too late and they have to grapple with serious behavioural issues throughout the child's teenage years and young adulthood. In the beginning, habits are like cobwebs but once they take root, they become iron chains. There is an African proverb that says "you can't bend a dry fish". Correct them while they are most receptive to it.

Pray For Your Children

Let your children see your love for God. Let them see you worship, sing, dance, read the bible and pray. Let them see you value and embrace Christian fellowship by going to church, prayer meetings and further meetings for learning like bible studies. Pray with them and pray for them. Have a family altar and meet together in the morning and or right before bedtime to pray, read the bible and talk about God and life. If you don't make these things a priority in your own life, why would you expect that they will do so?

As busy as myself and my husband are, prayer for our children is one of the biggest investments we have made in their lives. Even when it has looked like they are going so far from what we desire for them, when we can give them over to God, He meets with them in the way He alone can. More important than seeing us attend church services or preach to others, they have seen us consistently pray early in the morning before any of them are awake and long after they have gone to bed.

Too many people trivialize walking with God as a family until there is a crisis with the teenager and then all of a sudden they want that teenager to imbibe the Bible in the span of two weeks. It will not work that way. The bible's standard is that if you are diligent to train them up according to His word as they grow up, they will not depart from what you have taught them.

They need to be able to talk to us about the pain in their lives, their joys and achievements, their desires and ambitions, their friends, their struggles, their beliefs and why they hold those beliefs and they need to be free to ask questions. It's not enough to say "that is what the bible says". Try to answer their questions about faith and God and even when you don't know the answers yourself, ask other Christians around you. Pray with them that God would reveal the answers to them. Allow their questions to lead you to find out more about God yourself.

Remember that salvation is an individual journey and you cannot force it onto your children. You can pray for them, then you have to trust God with them and allow Him to draw them one by one. He is able to do it. Never give up on them.

I pray for those of you reading this, that your children would know the Lord Jesus Christ and love Him with all their hearts, soul, mind and strength. I pray that your children would live for His glory alone. That they would not give in to the pressures and temptation of the world, but they would cling to God and be shining examples of his goodness to their generation, in Jesus name.

Remember that overall, children are a blessing from God. They are not an inconvenience to your marriage but a sign of God's favor and blessing. This includes all children in your home - biological, adopted, step-children and half-children. They are all gifts entrusted to you by God and He will ask you for an account of how you raised them.

Dare To Be Different

If you have grown up with an ungodly example of parenting or fatherhood, you are not stuck living in reaction to that type of upbringing. You are able to be changed and transformed and you are able to change the trajectory of your family so that the mistakes of your father/mother are not repeated through you.

There is a story of a father who lived a very reckless life and was extremely abusive to his wife and children. He had twin sons who lived in that environment all their childhood. One of his sons grew up to be evil, reckless and abusive. When he was asked why he lived such a terrible life,he replied, "my father". He continued "He was the one who taught me to be this way. I grew up in a living hell"

However, a lot of his friends noticed that his twin brother was quite the opposite. He grew up to be an extremely well cultured and disciplined gentleman. He loved and cherished his wife and children and worked hard for his family. When he was asked why he was doing so well and how he turned out so different from his brother, he also responded, "my father". He continued, "I grew up in a living hell. I saw my father abuse my mother almost daily and treat me and my brother like garbage all my childhood and I made up my mind, that I would never be like him."

Choose who you want to be, choose the life you want to live and prayerfully break the yoke of your past experiences so that you can lay a new foundation for your children.

Part Two

Dealing With Conflict

Conflict and disagreements are inevitable. But you don't have to let the problems get the best of both of you. You can take concrete steps to turn things around today. But first of all, you have to acknowledge that there is a problem and deal with it quickly. The bible says "do not let the sun go down on your anger".

If you and your spouse refuse to deal with that conflict or to acknowledge it is there, it will become a cancer that festers, broods, grows underneath the surface and by the time it resurfaces, it can be deadly.

You cannot afford to think that issues within your marriage will somehow work themselves out like magic while you or your spouse refuse to address them. That is not going to happen.

Even the healthiest relationship will occasionally have unpleasant conflicts but if handled well, these conflicts will bring you closer together and not farther apart. Your collective willingness to navigate them together is critical.

In the next few chapters we will be dealing with some of the most common conflicts marriages face and I will give you both action points, so that you can apply what you are learning immediately.

7

Wrong Priorities

Most of us spend too much time on what is urgent and not enough time on what is important.

—STEPHEN R. COVEY

A lot of the conflicts that arise in a marriage begin to build when one or both of you begin to live with the wrong set of priorities. Let's start by saying that your written priorities are sometimes different from the priorities you live out. Everyone says that they have the right priorities and know the "right answer" to give when asked. But the use of your time and money will show you where your priorities are.

For where your treasure is, there your heart will be also.

Matthew 6:21

Jesus was saying the place you invest your time and money (the largest two treasures on earth) determines where your heart is. If you say you prioritize your marriage but spend every waking hour working, doing ministry and attending to the needs of others, or going out golfing or drinking or just hanging out with your friends, be honest with where you have placed your priorities.

PRIORITY SETTING
Personal Relationship With God

Your relationship with God always comes first. When God is first in both of your lives and you love Him more than anything and anyone else (including one another), your life begins to line up properly. So many times a lot of the other issues that come up in marriage take place when our hearts are not in the right place before God. He is the one who helps you set and live the right priorities overall. You need the love of God to be able to love your spouse and everyone else in the right way.

For God is working in you, giving you the desire and the power to do what pleases him.
Philippians 2:13

Spouse

This should be your next priority. Your marriage comes before your career or business. Your marriage comes before your academics. You are married before you are parents. Before you are business partners or in ministry together.

Spouse Over Children

Your children are meant to be a blessing not the ground for separation. Ladies, if you are so focused on your children that you have no time for your husband, you are playing a dangerous game. If you are never available because "you are doing something for Junior", or you both chose to have Junior sleep between you and your husband every night. Or you say no sex because "you don't want the children to hear the bed creaking". Friends, if the bed did not creak, those children would not be there in the first place.

Your children will not make it easy either. They are children. They think they are most important people in the room, naturally. You have to show them the value you place on their mom or dad. When you get home and are surrounded by your children, instead of spending all your time with them immediately, go and find your spouse, give her a kiss, acknowledge her and then turn your attention back to your children. Your display of affection for your spouse will not only show your children that he/she is a priority, it will give them a sense of security in knowing the home is full of love.

Avoid using your children as an excuse for not spending time with your spouse.

Spouse Over Ministry

Every Christian has a ministry. Whether yours is in the context of a church, itinerant ministry, volunteer service you do at a local community centre or sharing the gospel at your workplace. Your focus on ministry should come before your desire to make money but it should not take the place of your spouse.

If you are a pastor or full-time minister, do you take calls from sister Kate, sister Jennifer, brother Godfrey and spend two hours praying over their marriage while yours is falling apart from neglect? Hang up the phone, turn it off and spend some quality time with your wife. Give her your undivided attention, play a game or go out on a date. Do not act superficial in the pretense of being "holy". You chose to get married and God expects you to honour that choice and that spouse.

Spouse Over Work, School and Career

What is the point of working so hard to get money so you can buy gifts and necessities to make your spouse happy, only to lose them because you have no time for them. Do not be so busy and tired you can't sit and have a conversation with one another.

While you should be excellent in your workplace, your marriage must come first. You don't have to leave work every time your spouse calls, but you can call them back the first chance you get. You can send text messages on your way to the bathroom. Get home early after work. If you work around the clock because you need the money, I promise you, the money will be like sawdust if you lose your home. Jobs come and go. You only have one marriage.

Many of us have this entire priority list upside down. We serve our careers, our bosses and workplaces with our very best, then give all the extra energy we have to serving at a church or ministry. After which we try to give the dregs of our attention and time to our children and by the time you face your spouse at night you are beyond spent and unwilling to have any more conversation. You're too wiped to have an active sexual relationship, which is absolutely critical for any marriage to survive. You need to change your priorities.

How To Change Your Priorities

Do the things you used to do when you were first dating: Show appreciation for the little things they do, compliment each other (even if you've said it before). Some of you will need to take a step back from the busyness you have gotten caught up in to "see" your spouse again in order to give them compliments.

Contact each other through the day. Send random love notes, text messages, and calls. It may seem cheesy, but your spouse will know you were thinking of them. Show interest in each other once again. Ask how their day went, don't just come with your "honey do" list to start your conversations.

Another way to change your priorities is to plan date nights. Schedule some time together on the calendar as you would for other important life events. When other opportunities come up at that time, tell them you are unavailable. The last thing you want to do is plan a date night and show that it isn't a priority by double booking or cancelling last minute.

Always remember, your well loved wife, your well respected husband will be a better employee, parent and global citizen - all thanks to you. So do us all a favor - treasure and love your sweetheart so that the rest of us see them at their best each day.

ACTION POINTS

Write down your answer to the following questions-

- Look at the past week, according to what you have spent time and money on, what are your priorities? (It is important that you do not write down what you think they are but actually add up the time spent in each area).
- What are the values or priorities you want for your life?
- What is the biggest thing you can see fighting for your spouse's rightful place?
- Write down two action items you will be starting or stopping to set your priorities right in your schedule and wallet.

8

Lack Of Communication

Listen with curiosity. Speak with honesty. Act with integrity. The greatest problem with communication is we don't listen to understand. We listen to reply.

—ROY T. BENNETT,

The inability to communicate clearly and regularly is a common cause of marital conflict. Communication includes the ability to voice concerns as well as a willingness to listen. The intimacy you once felt can become very dim and muted over time when communication channels are switched off.

This one challenge is arguably the most debilitating cause of conflict because no other problem can really be addressed and solved without it.

BARRIERS TO COMMUNICATION
Not Accepting Your Differences

Let's be honest, some of you are like the Dead Sea, it takes an earthquake to find out what you're thinking. While some of you are like the Babbling Brook, even if your life depended on your silence you would probably be found whispering something to your spouse.

This is not a problem at all, as long as those of you who tend to be more silent are willing to speak up when needed so that your spouse understands how you feel about different situations. And those of you who tend to speak all the time give room for your spouse to get a word in when they want to.

Technology

Technology has also become a huge barrier to family communication. Everyone comes home from work, play or school and are sitting in different rooms on their iPhones, iPads, laptops keeping busy and maintaining relationships with people outside of the family. Even when you are in the same room, you both sit down and watch TV. Though for some couples this counts as quality time, you have to admit that it doesn't allow you to know where your spouse's heart is. What are they growing in? What is God teaching them? Where are they feeling frustrated? Put down the technology and have conversation.

Technology is great when it is necessary e.g. in marriages where you live in different countries but when it is not needed, put it away. Many people text or message their spouse from another room in the house instead of walking over and speaking face to face. Or try to resolve hard complicated arguments by text forgetting that messages do not show the full intent of their words. So simple messages get misread and create issues that weren't there before.

Unforgiveness, Offense And Bitterness

Do you believe there is a sin that your spouse could commit against you that you could never forgive him or her for? Well guess what? That sin doesn't exist. Biblically, the only unforgivable sin is sinning against the Holy spirit - and you aren't Him.

Marriage is about forgiving the unforgivable and loving when you feel your spouse is unlovable to you. I know you are thinking "Ok, yeah, but what about infidelity? Who on earth is going to let something as heartbreaking as that go?!" A godly wife or husband that wants to make their marriage work.

Am I encouraging infidelity? No. In fact, there is an entire section addressing that topic. However, we are all human beings, we all make mistakes and some people's mistakes happen to have a higher consequence than others. Do people fall into sin? Everyday. Do you? Most certainly.

The way you handle infidelity or other disappointments within your marriage will determine what becomes of it. I have counselled couples and seen husbands on their hands and knees begging their wives saying, "This was a mistake. It will never happen again." And some wives respond, "I will never forgive you. Get lost! I hate you!", "You will not have the opportunity to make that mistake again, I'm getting a divorce".

I have also witnessed couples in the same scenario where the wife has responded, "As hard as this is, you first need to ask God to forgive you, as for me, I am committed to forgiving you." "Once you can find peace with yourself, we will move forward." You can tell the different outcomes.

> *How do you expect to build a future together when you are constantly bringing up the past?*

This is not to make light of the process of forgiveness that those women and men had to go through, but the marked difference was their willingness to begin and work it out as opposed to becoming bitter and unforgiving.

Outside of infidelity, there are many ways your spouse will disappoint you over the course of your married lives. Forgiveness is something you do often and for yourself, and when you give it freely, your marriage will work.

Don't hold on to bitterness. For goodness sakes, stop regurgitating events that happened one, five, twenty years ago during arguments or at random times. How do you expect to build a future together when you are constantly bringing up the past? If you are finding it particularly hard to forgive and let go, read the book "The Bait of Satan: Living Free From the Deadly Trap of Offense" by John Bevere to help you learn this critical piece.

Sometimes when disappointments or hurts have taken place within the marriage, that spouse decides to hold on to them without saying how they feel and they build barriers instead of discussing the matter. Over time, a root of bitterness springs up, where every time you see your spouse, all you can see and hear is what they did wrong to you last week, or even years ago.

Unforgiveness and distrust taints everything that is said and creates mountains out of molehills. Malice springs up and you begin to nitpick at every wrong word, tone or potential attack. You become defensive and begin to lash out at the slightest thought of being under attack. Instead of giving in to bitterness, bear each other's burdens.

Let all bitterness, wrath, anger, clamor, and evil speaking be put away from you, with all malice. And be kind to one another, tenderhearted, forgiving one another, even as God in Christ forgave you.
Ephesians 4:31,32

Sarcasm

Just as damaging as a madman shooting a deadly weapon is someone who lies to a friends and then says, "I was only joking."
Proverbs 26:18,19 (NLT)

Some couples speak sarcastically to each other just for the fun of it. That's all well and good until one person says something that actually hurts the other. In a sarcastic environment like this, that comment is taken lightly because the general conversation in the house has regularly been derogatory and flippant. Sarcasm, much of the time dishonors the person that you're speaking to.

Let your yes be yes and your no, no. If you tell your spouse you're going to do something, do it. If you don't plan on doing it, say so, so that you are not building up small disappointments. They may seem casual on the onset but over time they become a big deal. Consider making a decision as a family to cut the sarcasm. Especially when you're talking about sensitive matters. Remember that something that seems small to one of you could be very serious to the other and that should be honoured.

Talking To Friends Instead

Many of you tell your friends things you should be telling your husband or wife. Begin to think of your spouse as your best friend. Share with them deep things as well as the much lighter matters that take place over the course of your day. Don't let your friends take their place.

This goes without saying but most especially don't let a friend of the opposite sex in on what's going on in your mind when you have not let your spouse into that space. To do so is asking for an affair and a broken marriage.

Choose not to listen to side talk and outsiders who have something to say about your wife or husband. Verify everything you hear directly from them and don't think for one second that your friends are out to "protect you" if they are trying to destroy your marriage.

How To Strengthen Communication

Express how you feel in an amicable way. Let's be honest in the moments of anger, hurt or disappointment the last thing you probably want to do is begin to come to a resolution. You just want to stew in your emotions a little longer. But if you maintain that you are "fine" how on earth will your spouse know that something is wrong?

Mrs., your husband cannot read your mind. What is absolutely important to you may not even have crossed his mind at all. This isn't because he hates you or does not care, God wired him differently. Tell him exactly how you feel. If something is wrong, say so. Aim to preserve the joy and peace of your home by being quick to forgive, quick to listen, quick to settle matters.

I remember when we just got married, and I got upset about something, I would stay up at night and cry while my husband would be sound asleep. Some days he would wake up to go to the bathroom, notice that I'm awake and ask me "Are you okay?"

"Yes." I'd say sarcastically but it took me sometime to realize that my husband did not compute the sarcasm. So he'd go back to sleep reassured that his wife was alright.

When he woke up in the morning and saw how puffy my eyes were, he'd ask "What happened?" But by that time I'd be absolutely furious that he ignored all my hidden signals and I would give him a full mouthful about whatever his offense was. He would then look at me amazed and say something along the lines of "THIS is why you're upset? I didn't even notice that I did that. If you had just told me I would've apologized." And sure enough, he'd apologize for the original offense right then and there.

Can you imagine that? A long night of weeping with many scenarios playing out in my mind, a massive headache all day, and he gave me an apology without me even asking for one. Just because he now knew what was going on with me. After this happened a few times, it didn't take me long to learn to communicate with my words clearly. From then on, I talked about my concerns and most of the time by the time I laid it all out, we would end up laughing. No more midnight tears!

The same goes for my brothers. Don't approach your wife in an accusatory or derogatory manner. If you're busy cursing her, her mother and the children she gave birth to, how do you expect to come to any type of happy resolution? Speak to one another in a loving and respectful way. Mr., figure out what your wife does when she's displeased and don't leave the matter until you have come to a resolution. If she says "all is well" but her actions are saying something different, press a little more.

> *Have at least one evening every week devoted to your spouse and family.*

Cut the sarcasm from your language. Begin to speak with honour and clarity and if your children have started that bad habit because of your example, apologize to them and teach them the right way to address one another.

Make an appointment with each other, put it in your schedules that you will take time to speak with one another this Friday evening. If you have church commitments almost every evening of the week, skip one of the services. Guess what? One evening may save your marriage and will not destroy your ministry. Have at least one evening every week devoted to your spouse and family.

Sleep in the same room. If you decide to sleep in separate rooms because of what a lack of communication has created in your home, you are almost sealing the deal to terminate your marriage. How are you supposed to learn communication by separating yourselves?!

Keep the pathways of conversation open. When talking about matters that are weighing heavily on you, turn off the technology, put the kids to bed so that you can talk freely. If the matter continues to escalate into an argument, see our later section on dealing with arguments.

Use body language to show that you are listening. Don't look at your watch, or fidget with the book in your hand. Practice active listening by nodding so your spouse knows you understand what they are saying. Then take the time to tell them what you have heard so that they can confirm whether you heard what they were actually saying.

ACTION POINTS

Write down your answer to the following questions-

- Which of these obstacles have been stopping the flow of communication in your marriage?
- Which of these points have you been doing well?
- What two things will you begin to do in your marriage to strengthen your lines of communication?

9

Money

Myth: My spouse and I shouldn't talk about money because it only leads to fights.
Truth: You can't have a great relationship until you can communicate and agree about money.

—DAVE RAMSEY

Out of the marriages that break up, close to half of them do so because of financial challenges and an inability to handle them properly. The first year into our marriage, my husband and I had a major argument about money. When I got back home I reflected on it and decided that that would never happen again. I knew too many couples whose marriages had been terminated just because of finances.

I woke my husband up and said to him, "Mine (my nickname for him), you know what? We are never going to fight about money again, ever. Here is what we will do. When we have money, we will be content with it and spend it. When we don't have money, we will pray and look to God. But fight about money? We are not going to do that ever again." And thirty years later, we haven't.

Both of you entered your marriage already preconditioned financially. You have been influenced by your parent's choices and how those choices affected you. You have made your own financial decisions prior to getting married. You built habits of spending or saving in your time of being single. For some who were in previous marriages or serious relationships, you may have built much debt in those situations and have now grown a strong aversion to debt.

One of you may be very serious about saving and living frugally while the other is a spending spree champion. You may be in a disparity of income where one of you earns much more than the other. Or have differing life goals where one spouse wants a fabulous and strong retirement plan while the other is more concerned about living life to the fullest right now.

Outside of these differences in financial ideologies or past spending habits, the pressure of paying bills, school tuition or meeting other financial obligations, can create an underlying anxiety that amplifies small unrelated disagreements and puts an additional strain on your relationship. Did you hear that? Avoiding dealing with the financial stress can spill distrusting, frustrated fumes into other conversations you're trying to have.

However your financial issues started, take a deep breath and have a serious conversation about them.

Dealing With Financial Issues

It is not about how much you have. It is about the ability to discuss and talk about your resources freely. It is not even about knowing exactly how much your spouse makes, or your spouse knowing exactly what you make. It is both of you having a heart towards God and consciously making a decision to give towards the needs of the family. That is what we have done over the years, we have given in our different ways which has fluctuated as we were both able.

Always remember life changes. Maybe today you're the husband and you have so much money while your wife is not earning much. Years down the road, you could lose your job or she receives an amazing promotion where she begins to earn much more than you do. The way you treat one another in your season of "blessing" can reflect on how you are treated when you are no longer in such a position. Though it should not if you are both committed to forgiveness and honouring one another. Either way, it is about mutual love and respect in handling your finances.

My wisdom key is not necessarily that you must have joint accounts, but you most definitely need joint accountability. You both need to be honest about your current financial situation. If finances has become a huge challenge for you, you cannot continue to live like it has not. Do not be unrealistic about your income and expenses. Downsize when you have to. Have you heard about keeping up with the Jones'? This is the time to forget all about them for you and your spouse's sake. For your children's sake.

When you are having this conversation, come in cheering for the family team. This is not Mr. vs. Mrs. Don't approach the subject in the heat of your anger or frustration. Don't blame anyone for your current financial state. Work together to see how you can move forward. Set aside a time that works well for both of you, when neither of your are exhausted from a long day's work or from dealing with the children. Pick your battles and hear each other out.

When my husband and I first came to Canada we were told that everyone takes a government loan to go to post secondary education here. We both determined that by the grace of God our children would not start their independent lives with debt. We decided that our children would leave college and university debt free. As parents we set up a plan for how we would share the burden of what was needed to pay. We taught them to make saving towards their education a priority. We also taught them to work hard in school, do as many extracurriculars as they could without negatively impacting their grades and to apply for available scholarships. Prayer and faith were running simultaneously in the background. Five children successfully enrolled in or completed their first degrees, our dream has become a reality.

Be Honest And Open

When you are conversing about your finances, never hide income or debt. My daughter once told me of a pastor that counselled her and her soon-to-be husband that he should always have a stash of money kept on the side without her knowledge of it so that "she does not spend everything he has". What foolishness. If a woman does not know how to curb her spending habits to keep her family from becoming bankrupt there is a much bigger problem present, that "hiding" money will not solve.

I know another marriage that ended up dissolving because the husband kept on racking up debts on the

> *Understand that both viewpoints on money and spending have their benefits, and be willing to learn from each other.*

side which was affecting both of their credit scores debts that the whole family would have to pay off together. Others have tried to hide huge student debt when coming into the marriage forgetting that you will both have to work it out together. This is not godly or loving behaviour at all.

Bring your financial documents, pay stubs, bank statements, insurance policies, debts, and investments to the table. If you have never had this sort of a conversation before or since you have been married, you may want to also bring including a recent credit report so that your spouse and yourself and both clearly on the same page with no surprises later on. When you see your spouse financially naked, that is not the time to become judgmental or attack their previous choices. That is the time to rally together and say we can do this! We can come out of debt! We can manage our finances together.

Acknowledge the way your spouse handles finances, is he a saver? Is she a spender? Understand that both have their benefits, and be willing to learn from each other. Construct a joint monthly budget that includes saving for rainy days. Choose between yourselves who is responsible for paying the monthly bills or split them up according to what you are able to do. If there is a bill you cannot cover, look into reducing how much you are spending overall.

You want to allow each person to have some financial independence by setting aside money that they can spend as they like. Decide on what percent suits both of you and release each other to spend that percent as they want. Investment and saving are critical part of a family plan. Though you may have pressure to give money towards your extended family, it is important to realize your first financial responsibility is towards your immediate nuclear family.

ACTION POINTS

Write down your answer to the following questions-

- When last did you and your spouse have an in-depth conversation about your finances?
- What are your financial long and short-term goals? Your spouse's?
- In what ways can you be more considerate of your spouse's financial leanings?
- Are bills being apportioned in a fair manner?
- Develop a plan for reducing your debt load.
- Do you have a plan for your children's education? If not, how can you begin to plan for that?
- How do you plan on caring for your parents as they age?

10

Sex

*Sexual intimacy is about relationship, the more comfortable
you are with each other outside the bedroom; the easier it is to
relax and the sweeter the intimacy!*

—NGINA OTIENDE

Sex is one of the top originators of friction within
a marriage and even spouses who genuinely love
each other are not immune. Have a vision for
yourselves to begin to enjoy your time of intimacy together,
instead of sex being a source of conflict. Within marriage
sex is good and should be a fun time that you both look
forward to.

In my years of counselling couples, many husbands
complain that their wives are refusing to have sex with
them. They cite her reasons as feeling tired, having

headaches, too busy, or that she cannot do anything because there are children in the house, etc.

However, this challenge is not unique to men, I have had an increasing number of women complain about their husbands depriving them of sex as well. It is interesting to note that a large number of ministers' wives are being neglected in this way.

Research by Denise Donnelly at Georgia State University showed that in a study of seventy-five married couples in sexually inactive marriages, sixty percent of the cases was initiated by was the husband. [1]

More To The Picture

I have also heard from those who give these excuses that there is usually more to the picture. There are many external issues that might influence sexual behavior in any relationship including past relationship patterns, prior abuse or hormonal issues which may be inhibiting your spouse.

Also, there are some internal issues which affect a couple's sex life such as a loss of interest after being married for a long period of time, differing views on it's expected frequency, anger and retaliation for something unrelated to sex or using sex as a 'toll gate' to manipulate your spouse. Generally, bitterness and unforgiveness also tend to stop any desire for sex in its tracks. Lastly, your spouse may not be able to enjoy sex because it is not being done in an enjoyable way for everyone involved.

This is not a matter that can be treated lightly as both of your sex drives are a normal God-given and very powerful force. If there is no sexual satisfaction between the both of you, its impact can be noticed and it can influence many other parts of your marriage relationship.

Do not deprive each other of sexual relations, unless you both agree to refrain from sexual intimacy for a limited time so you can give yourselves more completely to prayer.

Afterward, you should come together again so that Satan won't be able to tempt you because of your lack of self-control.

1 Corinthians 7:5

Let's face it, men generally have a higher sex drive than women. They need to touch, feel and hold. It is like a tonic to them. Genesis 24:67 said *"Then Isaac brought her into the tent of Sarah his mother and took Rebekah, and she became his wife, and he loved her. So Isaac was comforted after his mother's death."* You can be sure his loving her and receiving comfort wasn't because she was simply singing songs to him. Sex is an outlet for both of you in the stress that is accumulated over daily living as well as in particularly difficult times.

When done in honour for one another's bodies, it brings you closer together when you may seem to be drifting apart. Mr., Mrs., it has no substitute. Do not put your marriage in jeopardy. This natural desire must and will be fulfilled. Even if your husband is a Holy Ghost, spirit-filled minister, elder, pastor or bishop, or your wife is the same, they did not marry you to be celibate forever, so don't put them at risk.

Dealing With Past Guilt

Many people have brought the guilt of their past into their married sex life. Maybe you associate sex with guilt because you did not marry as a virgin and it was always associated with guilt before you got married. In these cases, repent for your past then choose to receive God's forgiveness. It is real and available to you. God has put your sin as far as the east is from the west, and now it's time for you to forgive yourself and let it go. It is okay to enjoy your husband/wife and marriage.

Sex Should Be Enjoyable For All

Make sure that your wife is very comfortable with anything you are doing. Do not bring unrealistic expectations and fantasies from your past into your sex life.

Let marriage be held in honor among all, and let the marriage bed be undefiled, for God will judge the sexually immoral and adulterous." Hebrews 13:4

Do not consider introducing pornography or other people as stimulation for your marriage bed. It will harm you much more than it could ever help. If you made the choice to get married, then enjoy the person you are with.

I Do Not Enjoy Sex

There are a number of women that I have come across, who tell me point blank, "I do not enjoy sex."After speaking to them, I usually find that they have been abused at a young age (and many of them had never disclosed that to anyone - including their husbands). Some women were told, while growing up that sex is bad even in marriage have not been able to break that barrier. While some others find sex physically painful. Or your spouse may have been unfaithful in the past, and you are saying you have forgiven, but cannot trust him/her anymore in that area.

One common denominator with a lot of these individuals is that they are too embarrassed to say anything. To tell their husband or wife, so they just keep trying to avoid having sex. Each of these issues have solutions that work but you have to first value your marriage enough to want to make it work.

Talk About It

The first thing you want to do is open up the doors of communication between the two of you regarding sex. You have to be willing to talk to each other about it. This may seem very daunting for those of you who are not used to speaking about sex in any context at all, but your marriage is the safest place to have these conversations. In fact, it is absolutely critical and necessary.

How is your husband supposed to know that a particular action is painful if you don't let him know with your words? Or that something in particular is more pleasurable than others? So many Christian couples shy away from the conversation as though it is taboo. People! God talked about sex in His Word.

Get over the initial "awkwardness" of the conversation and talk to each other. If you remain silent and continue to beat around the bush with different untrue excuses, you are exposing yourself to the danger of becoming intimately estranged and having that lead to other consequences for your marriage. Whenever you are discussing this, be considerate of your spouse. Speak in love and honour.

If you are experiencing pain during sex you should both make sure that there has been enough foreplay to prepare your body for it. If that does not seem to make a difference, use a lubricant to assist you. It is not a sin to use lubricants as husband and wife to help and enhance your sexual life. If a particular position is painful, say so. If a particular day is painful, talk about it in love.

Past Sexual Abuse

If either of you have been sexually abused in the past, find a discrete Christian minister or counselor that you can confide in and begin to take steps toward receiving healing in this area. Pray for physical and mental healing, The bible says in Jeremiah 8:22, 'there is a balm in Gilead that can make the captive whole'. Jesus is able to heal even the most horrible past experiences and bring both mental and physical restoration. Accept that what you experienced was not your fault. Remember that the man you are married to is your husband and not the one who abused you.

You can also choose to change your own mindset and decide that your past will not hold you captive. Encourage yourself with the truth that you can and will be able to enjoy sexual relations. This is something you can pray about. Ask God to help you to enjoy what He has given to you in your spouse. He cares about this area of your life and is willing to answer these prayers.

If you have tried walking through these steps and believe that there is an aspect of spiritual oppression that is now also hindering you from being able to enjoy yourself in your marriage,you may be in need of deliverance. If so, ensure you are going to a genuine minister of God who understands how to cast out demons in a biblical way.

For those of you who have been brought up to believe that sex is a terrible thing. It is not. It is not meant to be hidden and only done quickly in the dark. It is not a sin to have sex on Sunday with your spouse (believe it or not, I have received this questions a few times).

Within the context of marriage, you can have a lively sexual life without shame. Adam knew his wife and that they were both naked and not ashamed. The bible also talks about many other married couples who "knew" one another and not just for the purpose of procreation.

Dual Income No Sex (DINS)

I once went with a close friend who was struggling with infertility to one of her doctor visits. After going over the preliminaries, he informed her that herself and her husband were suffering from DINS (Dual Income No Sex Syndrome). I had never heard the term before that and asked what it was.

He explained a concept that is quite popular with many couples. He began by explaining something called DINK - Dual Income No Kids. Where couples decide they do not want to have children for some time at the beginning or even much later into their marriage because they are focused on their careers, schooling, losing weight and other life priorities. He then said that this has now also created a new accompanying matter where couples are so busy they don't make time for sex in their marriage.

It is a fact that sometimes you will get busy with life and

some days even up to a week you may not have time or energy for sex. However, it becomes a problem, when you are not having sex for weeks in a row, because of how busy you are. It may seem alright in the beginning while both of you have other life priorities, but what happens when one spouse is no longer focused on their career and needs sexual attention? The other partner is still in DINS mode and before you know it, that spouse feels they are justified in having extra-marital affairs to "quench their thirst".

There is nothing wrong with focusing on other priorities, as long as you understand that your marriage is one as well. If you wanted to live a celibate life while focusing on other things, you shouldn't have gotten married. But you did. So honour each other's needs and create time for sexual intimacy so that the lack of it does not cause you sorrow later on in your marriage.

Your solution is to first recognize and acknowledge as a couple, that you are currently living with Dual Income No Sex syndrome. Have a genuine desire to resolve the issue, begin the dialogue to figure out why you are where you are, and try to understand and accommodate each other's needs. Make time to have sex or as I said earlier, to make love. Spend time together without the intentions of sexual intimacy. Work to synchronize your daily schedules. There is no excuse for denying one another sex in your marriage, it is essential to expressing love.

Sex And Ministry

In recent years I have counselled pastors' wives who are feeling neglected sexually because their husbands are so busy doing ministry outside, that they come home and crash. This should not be the case. If ministry has you that busy, release some things and take a step back. For husbands who are living like this, I recommend you read, "I Was Wrong", by Jim Baker. He lost a thirty-two year old marriage, because of busyness in ministry.

Sex and Technology

For a lot of women, technology has become the biggest hindrance for their marriage. You get home and spend hours dealing with social media statuses, catching up on other people's lives, responding to messages and trying to build followers. By the time you are done, your husband is no longer interested in having sex and is sound asleep.

It should not be so. Learn to put your phone down when you are alone with your husband in your bedroom. Some people have found it helpful to leave their phones or laptops charging outside the room so that they can spend that time focused on one another. Yes, resort to the old school alarm clock for the sake of your marriage!

Dr. Donnelly also found that sixteen percent of couples fail to have sex at least once a month, a pattern she found predicated marital unhappiness and divorce.

Sex plays a major role in marriage separation and divorce if you cannot come to an agreement. It can lead to infidelity, resentment, pornography, backsliding and eventually a broken home. Especially when there is no communication about the obvious issues and it is treated like the pink elephant in the room.

Do not google your way to figuring out sex within your

marriage so that you don't end up worse than before you began. There is an epidemic of pornography that is destroying many homes and lives. If you are struggling with pornography, recognize that it is an addiction and take proactive steps to get free. Stop permitting it to destroy your marriage and get deliverance.

For an in-depth Christian teaching on sex, read "Intended For Pleasure" by Dr. Ed Wheat or "The Act Of Marriage" by Tim and Beverly LaHaye. If these books are not able to solve the issue, get professional help from a qualified Christian sex therapist to get to the root of, and resolve the problem. I have seen many couples including ministers turn around this area of their marriage after coming to seek help from myself or my husband.

Restoring The Intimacy

You have probably hurt and offended each other in this area before so this is where you get to heap your spouse a nice helping of sweet tasting... forgiveness. Forgive her for the days she made you jump through hoops to get to sex. Forgive him for his inconsideration in the past regarding your feelings about it.

If you are genuinely sick or tired, make it clear, but give a raincheck for sometime in the next couple of days. Both of you should prioritize having sex. Yes you are both busy. You are both tired and the days seem to run out of hand. Put it in your schedule if you have to. Some people think this removes the spontaneity, but you can still throw some extra spontaneous moments in for one another. This is to ensure it is not being overlooked completely.

Let the husband render to his wife the affection due her, and likewise also the wife to her husband. The wife does not have authority over her own body, but the husband does. And likewise the husband does not have authority over his own body, but the wife does.

1 Cor 7:3-4

If you plan on fasting and would like to abstain from sex for a specific amount of time, talk about it first. You cannot simply come home and announce that you are going on a 40 day fast and will not be having sex for that duration of time without consulting openly with your spouse. If your spouse is not in agreement to abstain for whatever length of time, find a compromise.

For husbands, make sure you have her consent. If she has made it clear that she is not currently interested or able, you have to honour that. Anything else is marital rape.

Also, remember that you are able to make love without having sex. You can give pleasure to one another without actually having intercourse.

Remember that men need sexual receptivity to feel romantic and women generally need romance to be sexual receptive. As long as both people are getting what they need, they willingly provide what the other person wants. However, when there is a lessening on either's part, that can trigger a pulling back for the other person. When this happens the best thing to do is talk about it!

Don't run to the finish line, take time to enjoy the trip. It involves touch, feeling, sound, variety in positions or places in your home, it is supposed to be fun - make it fun! No husband wants to sleep with a person that behaves like they are a log of wood. A woman does not want to be a hit, bang and gone job.

Remember, sex, brings you closer together, releases hormones that help your bodies physically and mentally, and keeps your chemistry and relationship healthy. It is a blessing from God to you, thank Him for it and enjoy!

Action Points

Take a break from reading the book, go and give your husband or wife a smoking six second kiss! Then come back and write down your answer to the following questions-

- Which one of you has the higher sex drive? The other person should try to help them by offering to have sex and not leaving them to initiate it all the time.
- Discuss with your spouse - what were your expectations for sex coming into the marriage? And at this point?
- Is there any part of your sexual relationship that is causing negative feelings for either of you? What is it and how can you both address it?
- Are you in DINS mode right now? How can you both prioritize intimacy in the busyness of your lives?
- Share what you enjoy and do not enjoy in your times of intimacy?

11

In-Laws

When you married and established a new home, you didn't leave your first home in terms of love or communication, but you did leave in terms of authority and priority.

—DR RANDY CARLSON

L et's start by addressing the myth that "all in-laws are terrible, especially mothers in-law". This is not true and believing it is a recipe for trouble. If everyone around you has strained relationships with their in-laws, it doesn't have to be your norm. You can have a godly, positive relationship with your in-laws. Believe for that! We'll discuss how to get there if this is a current source of conflict in your marriage.

When you get married, there is a period of adjustment

to each other's families. Everyone is raised differently and miscommunication is easy when you don't speak the same language. In a family I knew many years ago, the husband's mother would regularly come from the countryside to stay with him and the family in their home in the city. Every time he left the house, she would curse his wife and say nasty things about her. She would put her down and just made the woman's life a living hell.

> *The "conflict" between a wife and mother-in-law can be imagined but even a believed threat can eventually become a joy killer and marriage breaker.*

One day he came home early from work and heard what his mother was saying to his wife. He was very close to his mother, so what he did amazed us all. He called her and said, "Mommy, you're leaving and you're not coming back. When I want to see you, I will visit you in the countryside".

He added "You are always going to be my mother. My brother and sisters will always be my brothers and sisters. I can visit and see you all anytime I want. If I lose this woman, I have lost my life and you? You have already lived your life." That was the game changer for their marriage.

One day I went to speak on the issue of marriage in a church and as soon as I started talking about this, the host pastor's wife stared at me square in the face and pointed at her husband, the Bishop in a way only I could see.

After the meeting, she came to me for counseling. She said herself and her husband live very happily and have a great relationship but that any time her mother-in-law would visit, her husband would change completely. He would back his mother in highlighting all her faults and behaved like they were strangers.

In a situation like this, the appropriate intervention is to highlight what is happening to your husband, in a loving way so that he realizes what he is doing and the impact it is having on you and your marriage.

A lot of times the "conflict" or difference of opinions between a wife and mother-in-law can be superficial, imagined or non-existent but even a believed threat can eventually become a joy killer and marriage breaker if not addressed properly.

Let me just say this, I am yet to find a woman who has never over-salted a meal in her life. I have also never met a woman who has never been way too busy to clean up her house every single time it gets dirty.

Mr. and Mrs., remember that this is your home and marriage, and not either of your mothers. What worked for her for forty years between 1965 and 2005 just may not work for you now. Interestingly enough, some mothers-in-law are women who have had challenges or even had a breakdown in their own marriage due to having a dominating and domineering attitude. If care is not taken and you don't take decisive actions, you just may lose your own marriage as well. Even if your in-laws have had great marriages, remember that this one is not theirs.

Ask Yourself

Are you throwing your wife or husband under the bus when it comes to your family? Do you call and tell your parents things against your spouse? Their bad habits or things that annoy you? How do you expect your marriage to work? You are giving them ammunition and permission to use those things as weapons against your spouse! When you tell them about the things they have done against you, even after you have forgiven your spouse, it is harder for them to let go. You are shooting yourself in the foot.

There are some women who find every reason to complain about their mothers-in-law even when there is no harm intended. I have heard women complain about the smallest aspects of their mother-in-law's character and habits as though they are supposed to be superhuman and completely wonderful in order to be accepted or loved.

No one is perfect and you probably have some annoying traits they also have to put up with as a new member of their family. Also, whatever you look for, you will find. So if you are bent on being a victim and searching for ways she is overstepping her boundaries, you will find them. However, this will only lead to resentment and a rough relationship where it does not have to be. You can choose not to be offended.

Mention legitimate conflicts to your husband, and when you do, do not attack *him* in the process. You are both a team figuring this out, it is not you against "him and his family". Do not draw ultimatums like "it is me or her".

Husbands, sometimes, your wife just needs you to be a sounding board for how she feels. Even if you do not completely agree with her, this is not the time to become defensive or protective of your mother. Listen and think with her of a way to solve the overall picture.

Also, beware if you cannot make decisions without checking in with your mother. It is a sign of trouble, you must choose to leave your father and mother and cleave to your wife. Prayerfully deliberate with your wife, seek God for counsel and live your own life!

Sometimes the conflict is between the husband and the wife's parents. Particularly when her parents did not accept him thinking he is "not good enough" or cases where he does not respect his wife's parents. I must say there is no reason for either of you to disrespect the other's parents. Even if you disagree with them, do so respectfully.

Recognize that most interference from either of your parents is motivated by love. They want the best for you and your family. They want you to be happy and happen to think that their way is the way to do that. Give them some credit for that but still draw the line as necessary.

My First Birthday In Marriage

I remember my very first birthday after I was married. I was about eight months pregnant at that point and had previously decided that I was going to work right until I entered into labor. In the morning, my father called me to wish me a happy birthday and I just happened to tell him I was driving to work. He became quite upset that first of all, I was driving, and secondly, I was heading to work. Now, those who know me well, know that I really enjoy staying busy so this decision was my own choice.

What I did not know, was that my dad called my husband and told him off for allowing me to drive to work that far along in my pregnancy. Truthfully, my husband probably agreed with my dad's perspective on the issue, but the real problem was my dad's interference.

By the time I arrived home from work (I came home

early so that we could have some time to celebrate my birthday), my husband was really upset.

"Why did you report me to your father for something that's not my fault?" I was completely confused.

Eventually, I understood what had happened and what my dad had called to tell him while I was at work. At that point, I had to call my dad to let him know (in honour) that that action almost ruined my birthday and that while I really appreciated his love for me, at that point, I also greatly appreciated being able to take family decisions independently. Without having to worry about what our parents thought. That call both resolved the issue on the spot and I believe drew the line and stopped other instances like that taking place later on.

My Live In In-Laws

When I got married we almost always had members of my husband's family living with us, people from the church that we served and generally people who needed help. There were times when women in the church would bring over to my house the children they had particular difficulty managing, so that I could not only take care of them and mentor them for a season and many of them lived with us.

Needless to say, my house was (and still is) always full of people. This was a very different type of household from what my mother was used to and she didn't think it was the best option for us because she didn't think we could afford it.

She brought it up few times and each time I had to tell her clearly how much I loved my "full house". I made it clear to her that I had chosen him (and them) with my eyes wide open. And I was not going to make it an issue at all. Eventually, when she would come over to visit, she would bring extra food items for everyone, which was a huge assistance and more than the food, her support of my choice was felt and appreciated. Now, over thirty years later, I would still not change a thing.

Keep in mind, I am not recommending my "full house" to any of you. My main point here is this is your home, your marriage, your husband and your wife. You know what works best for you, do it!

What you consider criticism or interference in your affairs, may simply be an unwise desire of your parents to help you. If you disagree, be patient and try with love and kindness to win your parents over, discuss whether they have a point. If push comes to shove, boundaries consistently get crossed, they are always at your house and you really cannot deal with your in-laws, move to a distant country. I'm only half joking.

Discuss whether it would be beneficial for the sake of your family to move to another part of the city where you are able to live a bit more independently. Remember if you have children that this would also mean forfeiting the assistance your family has been to you. Only make this decision if both of you are comfortable with it.

Giving Gifts

Another sore spot that can develop related to your in-laws are receiving or giving gifts, monetary or otherwise. Be fair and honest if you have decided to give gifts to either side of the extended family. For goodness sake, don't give gifts or money to your family members without letting your spouse know.

Recognize that the needs on either side of your families are different so be willing to adapt. Also, if one of your families does not seem to have any needs whatsoever, be a blessing to them in some way. Discuss how you can do this as a family and you'll come up with great ideas.

Are You An In-Law?

Please let your children be. Give them the privacy, space and time they need to build their own homes. Let them make their mistakes and learn to overcome them - it is part of their maturing process. If you don't have to visit, don't visit. When you visit do not overstay your welcome. Don't make unnecessary and unfair financial demands from your children. Remember they have their own home to build.

ACTION POINTS

Write down your answer to the following questions-

- Has either of you been feeling frustrated regarding your in-laws? What is causing the frustration?
- Discuss with your spouse - what can both of you do to help resolve the matter?
- Are you being fair in the way you share gifts or spend time with your family and in-laws?
- Have you had the habit of "reporting" your spouse's downfalls to your parents or family? Apologize, then make a fresh commitment to stop doing it.

12

Chores And Expectations

My husband says I feed him like he's a god: every meal is a burnt offering.

—RHONDA HANSOME

Inevitably, there will be expectations that one of you has for the other that they are not aware of. It can be as simple as expecting them to wash the dishes because you cooked the meal, to larger matters like sacrificing their career to focus on raising the children. To avoid potential conflict, make it clear what your collective goals and needs are.

If there is a dream burning inside of you that you have been unable to work on because of marital expectations, share them with your spouse so that they can think with you and compromise to help you accomplish those goals.

Most people work outside the home, sometimes more than one job so divide the labour. Too many times the woman is expected to work full-time outside, potentially be in school, then return home to care for the children, help them with their homework, prepare the family meals, do the laundry and clean the house while the husband gets down time, does some yard work and assists with the children here and there. If you notice that your wife is carrying a schedule like this, make it a priority to take some of the load off.

For husbands that feel it is the duty of the wife (only) to clean your home, good luck! If you do not want your wife to die from exhaustion, give her a helping hand. Interestingly, you were happy helping her out before you got married and now it has become a taboo. Remember times have changed - there are no more maids or "house helps" that assist around the house. Helping your wife around the house does not make you "less of a man". It makes your wife love and appreciate you the more.

Also for the Mrs., if your husband is helping you around the house, don't be rude when he cannot do it for some reason. Appreciate what he is doing. Say "thank you," "Wow!" "I can't believe you did all that!" Your appreciation will trigger more assistance.

Some of you ladies have not even asked for help in a clear way yet. You have done the work, sulked around the house, kissed your teeth and are complaining bitterly in your mind. Break that ungodly habit, let your husband know what you need and give him instructions in a non-confrontational way.

There are some things your husband will love to do around the house more than others. For example, he may enjoy cooking and doing laundry but not doing dishes. Talk about it and take advantage of

> *If you have a dream you have been unable to work on because of marital expectations, talk about it then work together to do it if it is within God's will.*

his giftings. Some of your husbands have never lifted a finger in any of these areas before. Be patient.

Get your children involved in helping with chores etc. If at the end of the day, neither of you can handle doing all the housework, pay for a weekly or monthly cleaning service. Some families pay for someone to cook a large amount of food, which they store and use over the course of a week. This will also help lighten the load.

Like I normally say to my children when I am wiped - "I cannot come and go and die!" (Nigerian idiom that means I will not work myself to death). Neither can your wife. Give her a break. A day at the spa has never hurt anyone and she probably deserves it.

ACTION POINTS

Write down your answer to the following questions-

- What are some expectations you have had for your spouse that are not being met?
- Have you made them clear?
- How have you apportioned the home care and chores?
- Is one person currently overburdened?
- How can you resolve this and lighten the load?
- What do you both expect from one another?

13

Broken Trust

*Trust is lost by the bucketfuls, and gained by the dropfuls.
The only way to rebuild trust is by consistency over a period of
time.*

Someone who trusts absolutely everything and everyone probably has a psychological or spiritual problem. Your ability to decipher who and when to trust helps to keep you safe and alive! One of the gifts of the Holy Spirit is discernment. However, what happens when there is a lack of trust in your marital relationship? What happens when the trust you had in your spouse for years gets broken by an act they did or by something you heard but did not verify?

For some marriages, there have always been trust issues. It could be based on childhood experiences like not receiving adequate nurturing, affection, and acceptance, going through abuse or being mistreated.

The Question Game

At one of the meetings I hosted with a number of young married couples, I found that this lack of trust can be a real issue for young wives. During my meeting with these husbands and wives, I had opened up the floor for questions and one man responded,

"Why do our wives continue going through our cell phones all the time?", before I could respond to him a bunch of women spoke up and began to say "Why not?" "Why shouldn't we?"

Not wanting to lose out on the action, I asked the young women "Why do you think it's necessary to go through your husband's phone?" And asked the men, "Why is it a concern to you that your wife goes through your phone?".

Finding It Hard To Trust Your Spouse?

If you feel the constant need to go through your wife/husband's phone, check her/his email, her/his pockets, underwear and generally just snooping around, it means you have a serious problem with trust that has to be addressed. That is not normal marriage and loving behaviour and if no one else has told you that before, let me be the first. Your marriage relationship must be founded on trust.

I cannot imagine how draining it would be to consistently have to track your wife's whereabouts, follow the train of your husband's eyes as you walk down the street, stay up at night wondering who your spouse spoke to and what was said that day. That alone will drain any type of joy you could have in your marriage.

At the same time, if you have to hide your phone, passwords, emails, bags or briefcases, ask yourself why. What are you hiding?

Both unwarranted and excessive suspicion as well as secrets will drain and destroy your marriage if not removed. Unfortunately it can become a vicious cycle if one of you does not choose to let the buck stop at you. One person is constantly checking the other's information online, offline, everywhere. They are nitpicking every detail, conversation or unaccounted gap in time. This makes the other spouse defensive and that defensive behaviour triggers a desire to hide information. Hidden information in turn causes the other spouse to become that much more suspicious that there is something happening which they must find out. Can you see the cycle?

How do you break this cycle? If you feel something is not right in your relationship, talk to your spouse directly. *ask*! If you tend to be the suspicious spouse, choose to stop. If you tend to be the secretive spouse, go out of your way to open up to your partner.

Mrs R. and Mrs T.

The first is a story of two very close friends, Mrs R. and Mrs T. These two women were both married and over time,

Mrs T. had been sharing with Mrs R. why she was having some suspicions that her husband was being unfaithful.

One day, Mrs R. called her Mrs T. and said "I just saw your husband going into a hotel with a prostitute!!" That was all Mrs T. needed to hear. She was livid. She sat waiting for Mr T. to arrive at home and of course, he arrived really late that evening. As soon as he walked through the door, Mrs T. asked him "Where are you coming from?"

He began to say "I was stuck in a meeting at w-" and before he could complete his sentence, Mrs T. pounced on him with a tirade of accusatory words. "LIAR!"

Before you could say "Mississippi", Mrs T. had struck a blow to her husband's character and manhood. She continued by swearing, ranting, crying and telling him how long she had known he was cheating on her. All this time, he stood in front of her shocked and dumbfounded.

While she was in the middle of her tantrum, her phone rang again and it was Mrs R. She grabbed it to receive consolation from someone who had her back. Stormed out of the room and picked up the call. Mrs R. didn't waste any time when she picked up the phone, she quickly informed her dear friend "I am so sorry darling! I was wrong! The person I saw at the hotel was not your husband. But oh my goodness, he really, really looked like him."

Beware , some friends go out their way to slander other people's husbands sometimes for the simple satisfaction of seeing that marriage break up and even sometimes so that they can marry him themselves. If you think I am making this up, you are very mistaken. It happens, so take each thing you hear with a large grain of salt.

Talking With Shade - Appearances

I heard of another situation where a woman had been checking her husband's phone regularly and one week noticed that he had started communicating with a new lady. We will call her Ms. Shade. His wife became so upset and began stewing and imagining what could be taking place as his conversation with Shade continued over the course of the week.

One night she could not keep it in any longer and she blurted out, "After all we have been through together you are having an affair?!" Her husband was stunned at the allegation. He responded to her by saying "After all these years you still don't trust me? What on earth are you talking about?" She confessed, "I went on your phone and saw that you have been communicating with a lady named Shade all week and you are planning to pick her up tomorrow!".

Her husband started laughing and said, "Is that what you are talking about? I was so busy I forgot to tell you! My niece, Shade is coming over to spend time with us from Germany tomorrow. I can't believe I forgot."

His wife felt so embarrassed, and realized that she had just put her marriage at risk, by allowing distrust to cause her to accuse her husband, before she had received any facts about the situation.

Mr., Mrs., have you ever noticed that when you are ready to buy a specific type of car, you begin to see it everywhere on the road? Whereas before you wanted that particular type of car you never noticed it?

I always tell young women, you will always find exactly

what you are looking for. If you are looking for proof of infidelity in your spouse, you will find it. Even if you have to create it yourself.

What If There Is Broken Trust?

Trust issues can arise when one or both of you feel let down or betrayed by the other. This can occur from anything as diverse as infidelity to breaking what looked like a small promise or consistently saying one thing and doing the other. Generally, the more one of you feels let down the harder it will be to work through the conflict. However, it is worth it to help your spouse release the anxiety, anger and self-doubt that mistrust usually causes.

Moreover, unaddressed distrust can lead to infidelity, arguments, and eventually a broken marriage. But you are not a mere statistic or victim of your past. You can save your relationship and grow closer to one another. You are able to overcome your former experiences and trust your spouse again!

First of all, you want to admit that there are issues related to trust. If you're in denial you will never resolve this. Also, for Mr., it may be harder for you to show your emotions and express that you lack trust for your wife, but also put in the effort needed to change.

Now evaluate where your trust issues are coming from. Ask yourself these questions: Has your spouse ever given you a major reason not to trust him/her? Have they ever lied? Have they ever made a promise that they did not keep? Did they ever fall short on a responsibility? If your answer is no to these questions, then these issues were brought into the relationship from somewhere else that needs closure.

An open line of communication creates the environment needed for trust to be rebuilt. For example, if your spouse believes you are cheating on

> *Realize that everyone is human and your spouse will hurt you at some point. Even if they don't mean to do so.*

them because you are usually out late hours in the night, don't get angry about it, let them know where you are, send text messages often. Give them an ideal time that you will be back instead of getting frustrated and refusing to respond at all. These bits of extra information, and communication can help both of you put your fears to rest and maintain trust.

Realistic Expectations

Realize that everyone is human and your spouse will hurt you at some point. Even if they don't mean to do so. If the distrust is coming from past relationships, you have to address that issue so that you can put your past behind you. If it was between the two of you, then learn to forgive them, let it go and actually allow healing to take place. If you say you have forgiven your spouse but in every argument you bring up past hurts, you are not forgiving them like Christ forgave you. Let it go. For the sake of your marriage, choose to move forward.

Talking about it is only the beginning of restoring trust to your marriage. Now, you can both create a plan of action, discuss what steps you can take to promote trust once again. For example give each other free access to your cell phones, email accounts, and social media pages. Or send a text message when you're going to be working late or going out with friends after work so that there is no room for worry. Your actions will show your spouse that you care to change and will bring you closer together. For more on dealing with infidelity, see Chapter Fifteen.

Restoring trust to your marriage will not happen overnight. It will take time and small sequential steps to earn the trust that has been lost. Your united commitment to bring freedom and trust back to your relationship will reward you greatly.

ACTION POINTS

Write down your answer to the following questions-

- Have either of you being finding it difficult to trust the other?
- Was there a specific event that triggered the mistrust?
- Has it been addressed? If so, what steps need to be taken to let it go?
- Have a conversation about how you can restore and increase trust in your relationship.

14

Addictions

No temptation has overtaken you except such as is common to man; but God is faithful, who will not allow you to be tempted beyond what you are able, but with the temptation will also make the way of escape, that you may be able to bear it..

— 1 CORINTHIANS 10:13-14

Addictions hit the home hard. They are tough to overcome and hurt the addicted individual as well as the spouse and any children who may be in the picture. According to Dr Bob Navarra, PysD, a Master Certified Gottman therapist, "the toll that addiction takes on couples is reflected in divorce rates that are somewhere between 4-7 times higher than normal, with many divorces taking place after [the addicted person] begins recovery."[1]

A study published in the Journal of Studies on Alcohol and Drugs, showed that nearly half (48.3%) of 17,000 participants with a past or current case of alcohol use disorder got divorced at some point in their lives. [2]

Certain addictions like drugs, alcohol, gambling, and pornography can cause that spouse to become violent and it can really affect your finances and even drain your family savings. A porn addiction causes your spouse to feel inadequate and you to be consistently unsatisfied in times of intimacy which leads to the demise of your sex life. People who are addicted also tend to do things that are unacceptable in a marriage like lying, stealing, and betraying trust, which is part of what makes it one of the top conflicts that threaten to pull a marriage down into divorce. But you can choose and embrace the light!

For you were once darkness, but now you are light in the Lord.
Live as children of light.
Eph 5:8

If your marriage has felt the bitter sting of pornography, alcohol, substance or behavioural (e.g. gambling) addiction, there is hope for you. It is a long uphill road back to a place of trust and unity but if both of you are willing to go through the process of counselling and treatment needed, change is possible!

Firstly, you also cannot force your spouse to get help for their addiction. They have to want it for themselves. For the addicted spouse, you can't control whether your spouse is willing to work with you through your recovery, allow them to make their own decision. During the first year of recovery you may feel the pressure to end your marriage because of guilt and condemnation, try not to initiate any major changes, like ending your marriage. Focus on recovery and begin to think of what you want to do differently in your marriage.

> *Give yourself room to receive God's forgiveness and forgive yourself. Let go of the guilt, shame and regret even if others are unwilling to release you.*

Part of the twelve step program is making a list of the people you have harmed and doing your best to repair the damage that has been done to them, your spouse is part of that. Rebuilding trust can take days or even years. Your goal is not to go back to the way your marriage was before the addiction but to build a new marriage based on trust, communication, support and respect. If there were other issues in the marriage before the addiction started, address them as well.

Accept full responsibility for what has taken place and let your spouse know that you do. This doesn't mean it is all over, your spouse will forgive you right away and forget about the whole deal, but it does show him or her that you are taking serious steps toward repairing your relationship.

While accepting the responsibility, give yourself room to receive God's forgiveness and forgive yourself. Eventually, you should try to let go of the guilt, shame and regret even if others are unwilling to release you.

In the process of reconciliation, write down any emotions and desires you are feeling that are counter productive to share with your spouse. For example, if you have random desires to leave your spouse, you do not have to mention them to him or her. Have a journal where you can release such emotions and leave them there. Also, if you have been in a habit of lying and hiding for years, you may find it hard to communicate openly with your spouse at this point. Start by writing letters to him or her telling them what is going on and how you really feel and it will get easier over time to communicate with them face to face.

There is counseling available for couples recovering from addiction and this is necessary to lay a strong foundation for your marriage moving forward.

Summary of Practical Steps To Take

- Acknowledge you have an addiction issue.
- Consider the impact that it is having on your spouse, children, health, career and/or ministry.
- Decide it is time to make a change.
- Speak to your spouse and do what it takes to get free.
- Set specific achievable goals.
- Make it a prayer point, go for deliverance as well as counselling or therapy.

ACTION POINTS

Write down your answer to the following questions-
- Do you suspect your spouse has become an addict?
- What actions can you see that suggest this?
- Has addiction infiltrated your relationship?
- How has it affected yourself, your spouse, your children?
- Speak with your spouse about how to address the addiction and schedule a date to visit your pastor or a counsellor and get enrolled in a program.

15

Infidelity

Apologies lose their weight if you continue to do what you are apologizing for.

—UNKNOWN

Conservative estimates show that roughly thirty to sixty percent of all marriages (in the United States) experience infidelity at some point during their marriage(1). This percentage is higher than in previous years, mostly due to the Internet. With entire websites dedicated to assisting married men and women in finding a person to have an affair with, we are shooting ourselves in the foot and tearing apart God's plan for marriages.

I would like to address the assumption that only men

have affairs. There is an increasing trend of women having extramarital affairs, and in these cases husbands need to take the same steps suggested in this chapter to overcome.

But a man who commits adultery has no sense, whoever does so destroys himself.
Proverbs 6:32

The devastation, heartbreak and loss of trust that follow an affair are difficult obstacles to overcome and many marriages do not recover. It is the only grounds Jesus gives for divorce but that is not your only option (see Matthew 19:9). You are able to recover and become stronger than before the affair if you are both willing to fight hard to rebuild your relationship.

When an affair comes to light, first, process what has happened. Don't make rash decisions or create more damage to a precarious situation in your anger, hurt and disappointment. Share how you feel with a Pastor, ministry leader or trusted friend. You want a space where you can speak without having to receive any specific advice. The cheating spouse is probably unable or unwilling to offer the support that is needed at this point and their lack of support can then escalate your feelings of resentment.

Then, decide whether you want to fight for your marriage or not. If so, you probably want to get professional or pastoral help. This will act as accountability for the both of you to do the work needed to heal the damage that has been done. Navigating the pain and confusion can prove too much for the two of you to objectively do alone. However, there are many different schools of thought and different types of "Pastoral counsellors" on this matter. Make sure that the pastor is for your marriage and is not there to add fuel to the fire by counselling you to break it off.

What If A Child Is Conceived Outside Of The Marriage?

This is always an extremely difficult issue. What are the options? You can chose to save your marriage in spite of this. Please remember that the child must not become a 'victim' of the act of infidelity. That child had no part in how they were conceived and should be loved and supported through life like any of your other children.

If both spouses want to save the marriage in an example like this, there has to be a clear place for accountability in providing support to the child, that assures the spouse that the affair has come to a complete stop. Some couples decide to invite the child into their home and adopt that child as one of their own. Obviously, this can only be done with the consent of the child's other parent.

If the birth parent decides to keep the child, the spouse involved should keep all communication with that person limited to the care and upkeep of the child. Is the spouse formerly in the affair truly repentant and willing to cut off the relationship? Is the spouse who has been hurt truly willing to forgive and love that child? These are questions you want to address clearly at some point.

The root issue has to be identified, owned and addressed. Ask yourselves, what happened? What went wrong? When did things go south? How do we fix this? Some couples can actually deal with this issue without external help. If you can, by all means do so. Just ensure there is true closure and healing that has taken place.

Ask questions

The purpose of this is not to get more dirt on your wife or husband, but to understand what happened and how. As the one who was betrayed, you also have a responsibility to rebuild trust and intentionally choose not to ask certain questions, knowing the answers will not help.

Accountability

At this point, you want to be accountable to one another. The spouse that cheated should go over and above what is necessary to be an open book to their spouse. Be consistent in your words and actions. If you say you want to be trusted again, then embrace sharing information about what you're doing and where you are. Don't make your spouse feel weird or bad for asking.

If this was linked to pornography, consider installing Internet Protection such as "Covenant Eyes" to keep you accountable online. Also for the wounded spouse, this is where you want to begin to change whatever actions you may have also done that worsened matters before the affair.

Choose To Forgive

There will probably be layers of forgiveness that will need to take place and you may have to forgive as more and more information comes out. Remember that forgiveness is not a feeling, it's a choice. Forgive your spouse just as God, in Christ has forgiven you.

Take courage

There may be some nagging fears you feel like will this happen again? But you should both hope for God's best for your marriage and trust His plan. It is okay to enjoy your marriage again. God is able to give you beauty for ashes and joy for your pain.

ACTION POINTS

Ask yourselves the following sets of questions and then apply the six suggestions listed afterward in order to overcome, stay together and regain your joy.

Questions For The Spouse That Committed Adultery

1. I believe the first most important question to save your marriage is this - Have you decided to end this affair completely?

2. Do you take ownership for your choice without blaming anyone or anything else?

3. Are you willing to examine yourself to figure out why you made that choice? You may find underlying issues like anger, sexual addiction, pride, selfishness, impulsion which can help to pinpoint triggers.

4. Is there a repentance for the pain you have caused? This is different from regretting that you were caught, the fear of the consequences or being torn about whether to stay in the affair or return to the marriage.

5. Are you willing to listen to your spouse as they share how they feel about the affair? Are you willing to show compassion and empathy no matter how long it takes?

Questions For The Wounded Spouse

1. Are you willing to forgive your spouse, even if right now you may not know how?

2. Are you willing to be honest with your feelings no matter how raw they are? This is not the time to sweep your feelings under a rug in an attempt to "forgive and forget".

3. Are you willing to acknowledge the positive changes your spouse is making toward rebuilding trust and healing the marriage or would you rather focus on their continued faults or find ways they are not yet giving this their "all"?

4. Are you willing to examine how you may have contributed to neglect in the marriage or see other unresolved problems that allowed for the disconnect to start in the first place? Are you willing to take responsibility for the areas that were yours?

5. Are you willing to keep your home no matter what? Are the both of you willing to go through a process of restoration despite how much hard work it will be? You can come out of this with a better marriage than you had going in with safeguards to make sure it does not happen again, but it will take you full commitment. When the root issue has been identified and it is clear that you are both in it to work for your marriage, do the following

Some books that will help are "When Good Men Are Tempted", "Surviving an Affair", "When Godly People Do Ungodly Things", and "Love is…"

However, navigating healing after an affair is so difficult that I strongly suggest you apply the other lessons written in this book and pray and guard your marriage well, so that you never have to deal with it.

16

Arguments

Say what you mean, but don't say it mean.

—ANDREA WACHTER

Have you ever had an argument with your spouse and it becomes a major point of conflict but you both sit down at the end of the day and cannot for the lives of you remember where or why this animosity began?

The Very Expensive Bar Of Soap

The story I am about to share may seem out of this world to some of you but could be very familiar to others. I will never forget a family that we met some years ago in

Nigeria. They were going through a divorce and had the opportunity to speak to myself and my husband at a point. We had asked them to remember what started the conflict in their marriage and this was what they recalled-

One day the husband had just returned home from work and he asked his wife,

"Can you please get me a bar of soap, I need to have a shower."

She got upset and said, "I went to work just like you went to work, why don't you go and look for a bar of soap yourself?"

He responded "I'm so tired, I just want to have a shower and go to bed."

She walked down the hallway, went into the storage room and brought out the bar of soap. Then she returned to the living room and threw the soap at her husband.

It hit him and fell to the ground.

Shocked, he bent down, picked up the bar of soap... and threw it back at her.

You can guess where the conversation ended that evening. By the point we came into the picture, this simple argument about a bar of soap had escalated into divorce discussions.

A soft answer turns away wrath,
but a harsh word stirs up anger.
Proverbs 15:1

Occasional arguments and conflict are a part of life and normal in a marriage relationship. However, if you and your spouse are arguing so much that it is like living in a daily nightmare, if it is affecting your blood pressure, stress levels and has created a toxic environment even for your children, address the situation and break free from the negativity. If you both make an effort, you can look past the anger and begin to understand the deeper issues that may be triggering these arguments.

> *It doesn't matter who you marry, no two people are going to like the exact same things all the time or see things in the same way.*

That conflict could have been finished right there if the wife had said something like, "You know what? I'm really tired as well, can you please get it yourself?"

Or a simple "That's fine, I'll get it"

The husband could have responded to her initial comment with, "I know you've been at work all day, but I'm so tired darling, please help me." or "Wow, I know you must be really tired to say that. It's ok, I'll get it myself."

Yet when neither of you are willing to give in, you give the devil room to make mole hills into mountains.

You both need to remember that you are two different people with differing views. It doesn't matter who you marry, no two people are going to like the exact same things all the time or see things in the same way. As a matter of fact, you may have loved your spouse's difference of opinion during your courtship/engagement stage. Appreciated getting their feedback on matters and asked them to share their insight on things that interested you.

However, sometimes this difference in opinions will cause friction in your marriage. Naturally, friction causes heat and heat with much more friction can lead to fire. The difference in your opinions does not mean that you are unable to deal with each other or "stay in this marriage" like the devil and some friends may tell you. There is a godly way to deal with one another that brings harmony regardless of the circumstances.

The next time you notice that you are about to get into an argument with your spouse, try these tips.

Realize You Are Not A Victim

It is your choice whether you react and how you react. It does not always have to be an argument. While you can't control the way your spouse speaks or reacts however you are in charge of your reaction.

Aim For A Resolution

Make sure that your goal when you speak to your spouse is to find a resolution to whatever you are talking about and not simply to get them back for the way they spoke to you or how they recently mistreated you. Are you trying to resolve conflict or are you trying to spark more trouble? Are your comments accusatory, and meant to hurt? Take a step back and try again.

Don't Try To Outdo Each Other

For many couples, when they get started in an argument, there are no more rules of conduct. Items get thrown as well as harsh words that cannot be picked back up and pieced together. Think long term in the midst of your anger or pain. Do not purpose to hurt or outdo your spouse and "win" the argument by dredging up things that happened in the past.

Stay On Topic

Stop raising up things that are unrelated to the topic at hand, or matters that had already been dealt with. One of the worst things you can also do is use something your spouse told you in a moment of intimacy and trust against them in moments like these. Don't fight fire with fire.

Do not be overcome by evil, but overcome evil with good.
Romans 12:21

Change Something

If you notice that your responses have only been escalating the issue each time you speak, you have to take a step back and look at how you can change the way you respond. If arguments are causing you stress and unhappiness in your marriage, it is worth it to let the other person win so you keep your joy. James 1:19 says, "... But everyone must be quick to hear, slow to speak and slow to anger".

Just one small change can make a huge difference. For example, if you usually jump right in to defend yourself before your spouse has finished saying their piece, wait for them to be done. Honour their speaking space. You'll be surprised at how such a small shift in tempo can change the whole tone of the argument.

Set Up Ground Rules

Like the example just given, try not to interrupt until your spouse is done speaking. Ban phrases such like "You always ..." or "You never ....". Remember the story at the beginning of this section, timing is key. Is he exhausted? Is he already dealing with something? Is she tired? Is it the right time for that particular discussion?

We all know it is necessary to communicate with your spouse, but feel free to take a time out from the argument, and come back to the conversation when both of you have cooled down a bit. This key alone can change the tone of your conversations greatly.

Choose to take five minutes when things get heated for either one of you and whoever calls the time out from the conversation should bring it back up so that it is addressed within the next twenty four hours and not swept under the rug.

Apologize When You're Wrong

I know, it feels really annoying to do so sometimes, but it will introduce a refreshing amount of humility to your relationship. They may harp on the fact that you were wrong, but if you do this consistently over time, they will be more inclined to apologize when they are wrong as well.

Mind Your Tone
Watch Your Body Language

It's not just about what you say but how you say it. Your body language, the volume of your voice, and the tone you are using communicate a lot more than your words. When you argue, try not to shout or yell at your spouse. The more you shout and yell, it triggers a power match of who can shout the other person down or dominate the argument vocally. Not only is this type of argument immature, it is destructive and counterproductive. It is not pleasing to God and does not set a good example to your children who are bound to see and hear dad and mom "going at it".

If you can't "communicate" without raising your voices, go to a public spot like the library, park, or restaurant where you would be thoroughly embarrassed if anyone saw you screaming and discuss your matters there.

Cut The Sarcasm

We already mentioned sarcasm earlier (in Communication), but this is one of those times where you want to avoid being sarcastic as it absolutely degrades the seriousness of whatever conversation you are having and the way your spouse feels.

See The Big Picture

Ask yourself if it is worth the argument. So many times you fight about things that are really unnecessary. Look at the big picture of what your argument is about. Is it worth it? If not, breathe, take a break. "You can be right, or you can be happy." Choose to be happy.

Let Resolved Matters Stay Resolved

Don't nag or force an issue that both of you have already discussed and resolved. Forcing an issue is how Ishmael was born. As the wife, choose to submit if it is not a matter of sinning before God or life and death. If it is just a matter of preference, and you are at an impasse, give in to him. Sometimes you choose to give in on principle, when there is a disagreement that is not related to God's leadership for the family.

Matters like what restaurant to go to and the other small things that normally spark daily arguments. They made this decision not because they are weak, but because they decided to be servant leaders, like Christ. If both of you are actively looking for ways to submit to one another, arguments will be far and few in between.

ACTION POINTS

Write down your answer to the following questions-

- What actions have you been taking that have escalated arguments in the past?
- How can you change and begin to give a "soft answer" in the time of raw emotions?
- What other changes can you make to honour your spouse and ensure that arguments become far and few in between?

17

Abuse

Not all wounds are visible.

−UNKNOWN

buse is common but unfortunately unspoken of in the Christian community and I hope this section sheds light on this matter for church leaders as well as couples. Abuse is defined as any action that intentionally harms or injures another person. It is to treat in a harmful, injurious, or offensive way or to speak insultingly, harshly, and unjustly to, to revile and/or malign.

Major Types Of Abuse
* Physical abuse

- Sexual abuse
- Financial abuse
- Verbal abuse
- Psychological or emotional abuse
- Elder abuse
- Child abuse

Two Types Of Abuse Within Marriage

Michael Johnson, MD found that there are two broad types of abuse when it comes to couples. One is called "situational couple violence" and the other is "intimate partner terrorism".[1]

Situational Couple Violence

This is a type of abuse that comes up often in the middle of stressful situations within the marriage or family. All aggression, abuse or violence in a relationship is unhealthy but this type of abuse is less severe than intimate partner terrorism. It involves things like pushing, shoving, kicking, slapping, shouting, name-calling, etc., and usually does not escalate to more severe aggression.

It is usually equally done by men and women though men usually end up doing more damage and their aggression is able to create fear in the relationship. Situational couple violence is more about ineffective problem solving skills rather than needing to have complete power or control over the relationship. It usually decreases as both people get older and become more mature.

If you are facing this type of abuse in your relationship, you and your spouse need to recognize what is going on make it a prayer point and you can also take courses to figure out how to solve your conflicts in a less damaging way. Apply the lessons shared throughout this Part of the book for help in reducing the type of shouting and fighting that characterizes this type of home. If you are able to apply these changes, you will be able to eliminate this type of behaviour, avoid divorce and even walk in a happy marriage if you are willing to forgive each other for what you have done to one another while this immature method of problem solving persisted.

Intimate Partner Terrorism

This type of abuse is about domination and control of one's spouse. For the most part when I am speaking of abuse in this section, this is what I am referring to. It is usually perpetrated by men though I have seen some women exercise this type of manipulation and control over their husbands.

For some of these men, the major struggle is learning how to controlling their impulses and they may have feelings of hatred towards women in general. This type of abuse can be physical or psychological control. It can be sexual force or involve severe economic control, like not allowing the wife to have access to any money.

It creates fear in the heart of the other spouse who is usually also isolated from friends and family. They are made to feel guilty for what they are going through with thoughts like "It must have been something I did. If I didn't do ____ he wouldn't have done this to me."

In the cycle of abuse, there is usually a period of acting out where the person lashes out physically, verbally, or sexually and then afterward there is a calm period where they cajole the person that was abused with apologies and gifts like chocolates, flowers, clothing, promises that it will never happen again and so on.

A lot of times people are in denial of the fact that they are in an abusive relationship so here are clear markers of what it looks like. If a person regularly feels dominated, deceived, degraded, demeaned, dismissed, and unsure of their emotional or physical safety. If they feel fear, tense, confused or their body begins to shake when the abuser starts to act out, that's abuse.

> *A lot of times people are in denial of the fact that they are in an abusive relationship.*

If your social media posts are monitored, your friendships are scrutinized, you have to account for everywhere that you go (not in a "my sweetheart is just checking in on me", but "if he knows I went there, I'm in trouble"). You are definitely in an abusive relationship.

If a person has no voice or say in their marriage relationship. If you cannot speak up about things you disagree on, that is not submission, it is an abuse of leadership. If you would "pay a price" or face "serious consequences" for doing something that your spouse does not approve of, that is abuse.

Abuse In Immigrant Homes

Specifically, I want to identify abuse in immigrant homes in Western countries. Situations where one partner controls the immigration process and holds all the necessary papers without giving access to the other spouse. If that spouse controls the finances of the home, the friendships and relationships that are made. Essentially cases where a person is made to be a prisoner in their own home. That is abuse.

For more information on what abuse looks like, visit The National Domestic Violence Hotline's "Signs Of Abuse" article.[2]

All forms of abuse in are illegal and have the potential to result in serious criminal penalties. This type of abuse (intimate partner violence) usually gets worse and more severe over time. If you are the victim of this kind of abuse, seek help. Staying in an abusive relationship and keeping quiet is not healthy or safe.

The impact of both of these types of abuse is physical, psychological, emotional and even if the abuse is only targeted at the wife or mother in the home, it will also affect the children growing up in that environment if not addressed.

But She Caused It

The abuser often blames the woman for causing his episode of abuse. He may cite things like "she is always challenging my authority". "If she would simply listen to me, I wouldn't have to hit her". "If she didn't yell at me, I wouldn't have slapped her", "she provoked me" "If she would just do what I asked I wouldn't have had to yell at her" etc.

Understand this, there is nothing a human being can do

to warrant being devalued, controlled or abused by another human. It is never okay.

Part of how abuse continues is the abusive spouse tries to establish that the other person deserves to be abused. This makes the victim come back, begging and pleading as though it is her fault. And because the flaw is really not in her, there is nothing she can do that will fully satisfy the abuser. They will always find a new fault or reason to continue the abuse.

Breaking The Cycle

First she has to address the greatest problem that keeps most women in an abusive situation- denial. She needs to admit that this is an abusive situation and that she needs help.

After acknowledging the abuse, I encourage her to understand God's perspective on what she is going through. To know that God is for the abused and the oppressed. That He loves women and is interested in her safety and progress in life.

She needs to pray for her husband to be set free from pride, offense, anger, hatred or whatever else is motivating him. She should then try speaking to him about it (without being judgmental or accusatory. And certainly without saying "why do you abuse me?" etc.

She should say things like - "When you yell at me it makes me feel…", "When you try to control who I talk to you give me the impression that you don't trust me…"

This will help him to notice how he is treating her if it is something he has picked up from childhood or his youth and has never considered how it affects those around him. If he is willing, she can even encourage him to get help in controlling his impulses through anger management, counselling etc. However, if the abuse continues after she has prayed about it, mentioned how she feels directly to him, it is time to get external help.

Next, she needs to break free of the fear that she has of the abuser by speaking up about what is going on to a trusted person in her circle. Mind you, she needs to be careful about who she trusts and shares this with. Not all pastors or church leaders understand the dynamics of abuse and some of them can complicate the situation a lot more than help it.

She should seek counsel from people who understand the dynamics of abuse or people who are not under the influence of her abuser.

She should keep evidence of what is happening to her. If she is being beaten, she should try to take photos of herself afterward. Possibly keep a journal of what is taking place. Keep in mind, I don't mean wives are meant in general to keep tabs in their journals of their husband's faults. I am speaking specifically to abused women.

Where there is physical violence, it is absolutely critical that she develops a safety plan for herself and her children. What is a safety plan? It is a plan to get all of them out of the house and over to safety if ever her husband escalates to a place where she fears for their safety or lives. Where will they go? Who will she call? How will she contact someone if he has her phone. She should think these things through and have a plan in case she ever needs it.

If this is you, please understand that you are not alone

in this fight and you do not have to bear abuse all your life. You were not put on the earth for that. You have so much greater value than to have to live with that.

There is help for you!

I have to say this. If you are being abused, do not keep silent or you could end up in a casket. I cannot tell you how many women I know personally who have died at the hands of abusive husbands. Please, please be careful for your life and don't be naive about the extent that this can go. Sometimes the ONLY way out is to completely walk away.

If that becomes the case and you are afraid for your life, inform the police about the matter and get a restraining order so that the full force of the law is protecting you from being followed or threatened any further.

Even after the abuse has ended, the person who has been abused will need to walk through a process of counselling and reassurance. She will need someone to walk with her in her journey to recovery from the physical, emotional and psychological trauma.

NOW OVER TO THE CHURCH

Please keep in mind that I will be speaking about abuse in a very direct manner but it is not in any way meant to accuse the church for taking these actions, it is meant to help us see what to do if abuse is happening in our fellowship. I love the Bride of Christ and believe that we are called to be an example to unbelievers by having abuse-free marriages and parenting. However, there are some areas and churches where abuse is being handled in a very ungodly manner and I have included this to present some practical insight on what churches can do to help their members.

For far too long, leaders within churches are neglecting the very people we are told, in scripture to fight for.

> *For far too long, we have neglected to comfort the oppressed and abused and refused to hold those who are being abusive accountable.*

For far too long, we have neglected to comfort the oppressed and abused and refused to hold those who are being abusive accountable.

It is a terrible situation if ever a church sides with the abuser or counsels the person being abused to apologize to the person abusing them. Are you kidding me? Church, we can do so much better than that.

Abuse needs to be called out. Every time. The church needs to have a forum where individuals that are abusive can receive counsel and get the help they need to change. We do not have time for sugar coating, sweeping things under the carpet and whitewashing our homes when there is a huge cancer happening behind the scenes.

We cannot believe for the best without taking tangible steps toward change. It is time to look for real solutions to these sort of weighty problems. Let us stop pretending to ourselves, and saying things like, "it will get better" without actually addressing the root of the abuse and investigating what is really happening.

We need to remember that it is the devil who comes in to steal, kill and destroy. He is the true enemy. However, if someone is willing to allow him to use their body as an instrument of abuse to another human being, that person needs to be confronted.

According to the Canadian Women's Foundation at www.canadianwomen.org, approximately every six days a woman in Canada is killed by her intimate partner.

I hope you read that slowly. Every six days, a woman in Canada (not a third world country) is *killed* by her intimate partner. Despite the objections of some in the church who are ignorant to the grave danger of abuse, this statistic is one of many behind my stance that if a man or woman's life is in danger in their own home, he or she must leave.

Abuse cuts across socioeconomic lines, religions, race and culture. For those who don't know, it takes place in wealthy homes just as much as it does in low-income homes. Unfortunately there is no cultural difference between outside the church and inside the church. One in four Christian women suffer some kind of abuse.

The Role Of The Church In Abusive Situations

Recognize When It Is Abuse And Investigate It

Not all abuse is clearly seen by bruises or bleeding. Emotional and verbal abuse are two types of abuse that can be difficult for the abused person to explain or articulate. When you are investigating a case of potential abuse in the home, do so in a way that best fosters hearing the truth.

Meet With The Individuals Separately

Church leaders and counsellors are only likely to get a

true statement of what is happening if you meet the individuals separately. If you have never been abused before, you may not understand how traumatic it is for that person and how much they feel under the control of and afraid of their abuser.

In a counselling setting and professionally in my work environment, I have had to deal with many women who have been abused. It is extremely difficult if not impossible for them to be in the same room as their abuser and tell you the story of what happened. Abusers give signals to their victims like a look, a particular movement of their hand, even how they hold a book or their bible. Signals that tell the victim – "I will get you when we get home." It is not at all practical therefore for you to try to ascertain "what is really going on" by having a joint meeting initially.

Recognize That An Abusive Person Is Usually Manipulative

You may encounter a case where a husband is accusing his wife of beating him. Yet when you dig a little further, you find that he had been verbally and emotionally abusive to her, and she responds by pushing him to get away from him, or even hits him out of frustration.

In a case like this, if you are not careful to listen and read between the lines, you would label the person who is being abused regularly as the abusive person in that situation and correct them for their treatment of their spouse, re-affirming the abuser's secret claims that there is nowhere for them to go to be heard.

A controlling person or abusive person can be almost professional in the way they carry out their accusations against the person that is being abused in the home. In this example what you actually have on your hands is someone who is controlling and abusive and an individual who is resisting abuse.

Do Not Take Sides With The Abuser

For God's sake, the church leaders should not stand with the abuser just because he or she is a major source of income to the church, a person in ministry like a Pastor, Elder or Deacon(ness) or someone they know well and see doing good things in the community.

Wake up church! There are many, many of these type of people who are wreaking havoc in the privacy of their homes on their husbands, wives and or children. They are given a free reign even when the warning signs are all over because "Brother Philip is so anointed. He has such a relationship with God".

All this because Brother Philip can function in a level of gifting or anointing. Please look objectively at that person's character and if there is abuse happening, hold them accountable for it and take it very seriously.

Understand That There Is No Justification For Abuse

There is absolutely no reason any person can give for beating or hitting another person physically, taking advantage of them sexually, or putting them down and devaluing them verbally and emotionally. It does not matter what that person says the other did to trigger them. Please hear me and hear me clearly. That person has to be accountable for their own actions before God and the church and not be able to deflect the blame onto the person they have abused. That is the pattern of abusive people.

They blame the abused person for the things they do to them and I see over and over the person being abused going to the abuser to apologize for triggering them. Even if you as a leader see this happening, the worst thing you can do is agree with the abuser and tell the person who is being abused to apologize to their abuser for "triggering" them. Make sure the abuser takes responsibility for his or her actions.

Do Not Allow The Abuser To Use The Bible As A Crutch

Statements like · "I just need her to do what I say, if she did what I said, I wouldn't have to beat her" or "She never listens to me, she needs to be obedient." Listen to the statements and ask yourself if it sounds like it is coming from a place of love or from a desire to control another human being. Listen not just for quoted scripture, but scripture quoting that is being fueled by ungodly pride and domination.

Using scriptures to justify abuse is a blatant misuse of the word of God. It is ungodly men and evil cultures, that says a woman can be beaten into subjection! Please do not put that on Jesus Christ who loved and honoured the women around him. Jesus Christ who in an age where women were seen as simple property, in a culture that said they had no value, taught and and showed love to women around Him. Jesus who allowed them to "sit at his feet" and be taught by Him when other Rabbi's only had them serve food. Jesus who received provision from women around him. Jesus who healed women, called them "daughter" and ministered to them. Jesus who protected them even when they were in the wrong and others wanted to kill them.

That is what Jesus did when he was on the earth, so any man that wants to treat a woman otherwise "in Jesus' name" must be corrected and told the truth.

Strengthen and Comfort The Abused

Let the person being abused know that you sympathize with what they are going through even if you have never been through it yourself. Do not judge or condemn them as being a stubborn, disobedient and non-submissive wife that "can't keep her husband happy."

Certainly do not ask them to apologize for being abused, or ever impress on them that they deserved to be abused. This is the same tactic abusers use to keep their victims in subjection. Like I've said numerous times, nobody deserves to be abused.

Recognize That Men Can Also Be Victims Of Abuse

Sometimes the church is so focused on the abuse of women that we fail to acknowledge that men are also victims of abuse. During the rise of feminism there has also been a rise in abuse of husbands. Some husbands are trapped in a living hell particularly because they are too embarrassed to express what they are going through. Some women take advantage of their husbands who are in ministry because they believe they have no recourse. When this is recognized it must be addressed.

Look For Real And Practical Solutions

It is not enough for a man to say "I will not do this again". This is not kindergarten where they apologize to each other, and go home separately. Remember that this person is living in this environment every day while you go to the safety of your own home.

When needed, correct the person in love. Do not run into judgment and criticism immediately. Listen to both sides and put in a clear plan for counselling and restoration. Remember that pride and ego are usually at the centre of abuse, not anger. Anger is the fruit of deeper issues that are happening inside.

ACTION POINTS

1. Pastor and counsellors educate themselves about abuse. It may not just be a "disappointing" or "difficult" marriage.

2. Expose abuse by preaching and teaching about what it is during co-ed and gender specific events and services.

3. Hold the controlling and abusive person accountable.

4. Be humble and honest with yourselves as leaders. If the level of counselling a couple needs is beyond the church's expertise, be willing and prepared to suggest that to them and refer them to more professional help.

5. Acknowledge the process and journey of ending abuse. It starts with acknowledgement, confession, counselling and making a conscious effort to turn away from it. It is also a matter of prayer and deliverance, as a

lot of abuse is perpetuated by people who have suffered abuse themselves. People who have grown up in or around abuse. This would have normalized it for that individual. Prayer and deliverance ministration as well as being baptized in the power of the Holy Spirit will make a change. However, remember that being set free from abusive behaviour is not a one-shot repair job, it will be a journey.

18

External Hardships

The difference between stumbling blocks and stepping stones is how you use them.

—UNKNOWN

This is here because although external hardships are not an internal conflict, it is a challenge that every marriage will face. We cannot avoid hardships in life. There will be inevitable disappointments, financial hardship, loss of friends and family members and many more situations that cannot be penned down here.

When you encounter external hardships, remember to address them with a united front. Do not turn against one another. Instead support and encourage one another. When life throws lemons at both or either of you come together and make lemonade.

Like the quote above, turn what looks like stumbling blocks in your lives into stepping stones to a greater and better future for your marriage and family. Perspective is everything.

Pray together, crack jokes, have sex, talk it through and trust God for better. Remember "tough times don't, last only tough people do."

Jesus will make a way for you, He is an expert at turning hopeless looking situations around.

19

Divorce Is Not A Solution

In every marriage more than a week old, there are grounds for divorce. The trick is to find, and continue to find, grounds for marriage.

—ROBERT ANDERSON

Every 13 seconds, there is a divorce in America. That means there are 277 divorces per hour, 6,646 divorces per day, 46,523 divorces per week, and 2,419,196 divorces per year. So in the same time it takes for a couple to recite their wedding vows, 9 wedding vows are broken (1).

There are very many reasons people give for getting divorced from a lack of commitment, to too many arguments, infidelity, believing they got married too young etc. Some other reasons are having unrealistic expectations, lack of equality in the relationship, a lack of preparation for marriage and finally, abuse. Some people believe that the government laws and ease of access to divorce lawyers are what make it so widespread but that is a lie. Divorce is widespread because couples choose to get divorced.

I have included this chapter co-written with my husband Pastor Amos Dada for those considering divorce to help you to see a bigger perspective and give you hope and wisdom for resuscitating your marriage.

What Does The Bible Have To Say?

"And said, 'For this reason a man shall leave his father and mother and be joined to his wife, and the two shall become one flesh'? So then, they are no longer two but one flesh. Therefore what God has joined together, let not man separate."
Matthew 19:5-6

Many of us have heard this sentence at weddings probably including your own. The statement here, "let not man separate" is not only targeted at outsiders but the stakeholders within the marriage as well!

Understand this, the bible said clearly that offenses would come. The fact that your spouse has offended you is not an excuse for divorce. We have already discussed the ability to forgive your spouse.

God has said very clearly in Malachi 2:6 that he hates divorces. That is a very strong sentiment that we shouldn't take lightly or ignore. This matter is so key to God's desires for your marriage that Jesus echoed it in Matthew 19 when the Pharisees came to ask him if they could divorce their wives for any and every reason.

4 "Some Pharisees came to him to test him. They asked, "Is it lawful for a man to divorce his wife for any and every reason?"

"Haven't you read," he replied, "that at the beginning the Creator 'made them male and female,'

5 and said, 'For this reason a man will leave his father and mother and be united to his wife, and the two will become one flesh'?

6 So they are no longer two, but one flesh. Therefore what God has joined together, let no one separate."

7 "Why then," they asked, "did Moses command that a man give his wife a certificate of divorce and send her away?"

8 Jesus replied, "Moses permitted you to divorce your wives because your hearts were hard. But it was not this way from the beginning.

9 I tell you that anyone who divorces his wife, except for sexual immorality, and marries another woman commits adultery."

10 The disciples said to him, "If this is the situation between a husband and wife, it is better not to marry."

11 Jesus replied, "Not everyone can accept this word, but only those to whom it has been given.

12 For there are eunuchs who were born that way, and there are eunuchs who have been made eunuchs by others—and there are those who choose to live like eunuchs for the sake of the kingdom of heaven. The one who can accept this should accept it."

Matthew 19:4-12

Being Christian means you have chosen a call to a higher standard of living than others. While they can take the easy way out of dealing with the conflicts in their marriages, you are to commit yourself to seriously living in obedience to God's word and bringing your marriage into that same submission to His word as well.

When the Pharisees heard that they would have to actually stick to their commitment to one woman upon marriage, they toyed with the idea of not ever getting married at all and Jesus responded by saying that, that really is an option. And people have done that before and are living as eunuchs today. However, you have already chosen to go into your marriage, you cannot act like you did not make that commitment before the Lord.

Practical Tips For Couples Contemplating Divorce

Two are better than one, because they have a good return for their labor:
If either of them falls down, one can help the other up.
But pity anyone who falls and has no one to help them up.
Also, if two lie down together, they will keep warm. But how can one keep warm alone?
Though one may be overpowered, two can defend themselves.
A cord of three strands is not quickly broken.
Ecclesiastes 4:9-12

Salvage Your Marriage

Do whatever you can to pick up the broken and fragmented pieces of your marriage, your spouse's emotions and work together to save your marriage! Don't allow any excuse to cause you to "let it go".

Look Inward

Take time to see what you have done to bring your marriage where it is today.

Search me, O God, and know my heart: try me, and know my thoughts: And see if there be any wicked way in me, and lead me in the way everlasting.
Psalm 139:23,24

Ask God for the grace to be humble enough to admit your mistakes and the wisdom and self-discipline to correct them. Stop focusing on the faults of your spouse. You are supposed to be help mates to one another not 'hunt-mates'. Saving your marriage is not going to be about your spouse fixing themselves and getting themselves on track. Stop putting that emphasis of repair and correction on them. Remember that it takes two to tango.

Your Marriage Is No Longer In Trial And Error

Your engagement, courtship and dating period were your trial and error days. The moment you said "I do", you stopped trying and started doing. Before your wedding day, you could have ended the relationship with no consequence before God (outside of the normal heartbreak and other minor complications that sometimes come from a broken relationship). However, at this point, you have committed yourself to this one person for life. "To have and to hold from this day forward, for better, for worse, for richer, for poorer, in sickness and in health, to love and to cherish, till death you do part, according to God's holy law, and this was your solemn vow."

See Your Marriage As A Covenant Not A Contract

Many people are used to that buyer's remorse policy that says, if you have bought goods or items and eventually figure out that it isn't working well or found a better deal, you can return the item to the seller. In God's perspective, your marriage is a covenant. Which means that irrespective of the faults of the other person, you are to maintain your part of the covenant.

That is exactly what He has done for us over and over again. We are not faithful to God hundred percent of the time. Yet He remains true to the covenant that He made with us on the cross of Jesus Christ and that is the way He expects us to remain faithful to our spouse even in your shared weaknesses.

> "Love Is A Feeling
> To Be Learnt"
>
> —Walter Trobisch.

Choose To Love Your Spouse Actively

Love is more than being tolerant of them. Love is choosing to enjoy them, be patient, be long suffering, forgive, consider and think of them often. Pray for, submit to and be willing to compromise when you don't agree.

If you are reading this list and thinking, I don't know where to start in trying to be patient and loving with my spouse, God is able to help you. The power of the Holy Spirit is real and if you are a christian, you cannot accept godliness but deny His power to change your heart. Read about what love is and looks like in the bible, then ask God for the grace to be a reflection of that to your spouse.

You go to school to learn engineering, accounting, nursing and other occupations. The Word of God and His church is a place for you to learn principles of marriage, home building, how to love your wife, how to submit to your husband, how to raise your children, how to relate with your in-laws, how to contribute to your community.

Attend church and read the bible regularly, put what you are hearing and reading into practice and choose to be a follower of Jesus Christ by not always doing what is most convenient or comfortable for you.

Divorce Will Not Solve The Problem(s)

Note this, divorce is not a solution to any character, spiritual, physical, financial or spiritual issue. It is a diversion. It is a postponement and creator of many more complex problems. How many people have gotten divorced from one person thinking that it was that relationship but after getting remarried ended up in the same fire and with one or even more divorces.

Don't think that things would be better with someone else. Unless you address problems, the same lack of skills that get in the way now will still be there and still cause problems no matter what relationship you're in.

Don't think the grass is greener on the other side, the other side just has different weeds and you are going to have to learn to pull them out regardless. It is only a dry fish that is difficult to bend. The problem or challenge you have now is a fresh fish which by God's grace and with a little sense of responsibility you can eventually solve.

Beware of Marriage Killers And Avoid Them

Just like in many homes there are cockroaches, mice, rodents, spiders or cobwebs, there are also marriage killers in every marriage. When you spot unwanted insects in your house, you don't abandon your house. You get rid of the insects! So get rid of the marriage killers in your home - get rid of anger, infidelity, lack of communication, unloving behaviour, drunkenness, prayerlessness, lying, lack of respect, mismanagement of funds, indiscretion, laziness, indolence, selfishness and the like.

Think About The Consequences

Before you think of divorcing your spouse, think solemnly about the consequences of that decision on both of you as well as your children and your generations yet unborn. Divorce is one way that the enemy is able to start a cycle of generational curses and emotional issues especially when there are children involved.

Many people acknowledge that the divorce "will be hard for the children". They know that they could be contributing to the destruction of their own children's futures (marriages and otherwise) and they don't care enough to allow that to turn them around. Instead, they talk about it, shake their heads solemnly and go ahead to do what they feel is the best option for them.

Even if your children have had to deal with your constant arguments, the better solution is for you to resolve those issues and show them what a godly marriage looks like, not to divorce and show them your unwillingness to make it work.

Get Godly Counsel

Seeking counsel from a Pastor or Christian marriage counselor is a biblical thing to do (Proverbs 19:20). Getting counseling is an excellent way to clear misconceptions about marriage roles, to see a situation from another viewpoint, and to distinguish between God's standards and those of the world.

Go to a pastor or church leader that is interested your marriage's survival, not one that is flippant about divorce.

You Can Change

Not everything is permanent. When you are choosing to salvage your marriage, it means that you will have to change things up. That's fine. Be willing to accept the changes to your lives that need to come in order to save your marriage.

If you have a problem with your character or there is a particular habit of yours that is amplifying the problems, don't tell your spouse "that is the way I was born", "I'm just wired that way" or "Everyone in my family does things that way, just get over it". No! What your spouse is highlighting to you, that you are calling 'just nagging' about is something that hurts him/her. Make every effort to change in order to please God and your spouse.

The Holy Spirit is not just good at helping you speak in tongues within your church. He had enough power to raise Jesus from the dead! And that same power works in you to change you and make you more like Him. He is able to help you change in a way that will be profitable for you and your marriage. Get to know this power, exercise it and release it for the use of your marriage. The Holy Spirit changed Moses, David, Peter, Paul, he can change you.

"In the same way, the Spirit helps us in our weakness"
Romans 8:26

In conclusion, no one gets married with the intention of getting divorced. When you see problems coming up consistently, don't wait until they are beyond fixing before you address them. Go for marriage counseling, go on a vacation with just the two of you, or try to get an addicted spouse into rehabilitation program. Give your marriage your all.

If you have already divorced your spouse, as much as is possible, try to make amends and reconcile with them. Many people have been able to reconcile even after years of divorce and make their marriage work.

If you are in the process of divorce, run away from it. Even if it is already in the courts, give your marriage a second chance.

If you have not divorced , don't joke about separating or divorcing your spouse. Let it be a word that is never mentioned in your home.

If you are not yet married, don't rush into marriage because you cannot rush out. Take your time in choosing the right partner that you are willing to commit to and pay the price for a successful marriage.

I pray for those who are irreversibly divorced that they would not walk under condemnation but would receive the love, joy and healing of our Lord. I pray that the Lord will free you from all anger, hostility, unforgiveness and revenge. I pray that all generational curses be broken and God will give you the grace to move on in life and in faith. Be encouraged, the blood of Jesus is stronger than divorce.

20

Final Nuggets For a Lasting, Happy Marriage

A successful marriage requires falling in love many times,
always with the same person.

—MIGNON MCLAUGHLIN

Phew! We have been through much in our time together and I wanted to end by giving you some short general keys that will help you maintain your honeymoon status "until death do you part".

Keep Your Focus On Christ

Keep Jesus Christ as the focal point of your marriage and family. Pray together often and obey His leadership.

"The greatest legacy one can pass on to one's children and grandchildren is not money or other material things accumulated in one's life, but rather a legacy of character and faith." Billy Graham

Be One Another's Cheerleaders

Celebrate and encourage each other in your ups and downs. Never allow jealousy or competition to come in between you. If one of you wins, you both win. If one of you is not doing well, it affects the both of you as well.

When you are hit by life's battles, link arms and get at it together. As hard as it may become, don't turn against each other or start the blame game. It will not help you win.

Love And Respect One Another

Be genuine in your love for one another. Both in your words and actions. Show each other respect and submit to one another. Husband, love your wife and don't use harsh words or yell at her. Wife, respect your husband and don't pull down his self-confidence, it is hard to build it back up.

Don't be selfish. This goes without saying, but if you choose to put your spouse above and before yourself, you will both be happier for it.

Handle Your Finances Well

Brothers provide for your home. Sisters do what you can to contribute as well. Discuss financial issues as a team. Don't just argue about money, plan for your lives together.

For example, Mrs. do you really need that new bag? Mr. Did you just tell your wife you don't have a dime and 10 minutes later sent $500 to your mother? How did she know? Because you forgot the Western Union receipt in the pants you asked her to help you dry clean and pay for because you are "broke".

In other financial matters, invest, live within your means, give to God and leave a legacy for your children.

Get Healing Where Needed

For marriages that need healing, give yourselves the space, time and actions needed to heal. The transformation coming to your marriage is a process, it is not instantaneous. But embrace that process and be willing to work together. Remember that you are on the same team!

Take Vacations

Take at least one vacation each year (without the children). Where you can both rest and check in with one another to see if there are any concerns or issues that have built up in your relationship. Take some time in this retreat/vacation to have fun and do absolutely nothing! Then also spend some time in prayer listening to God's directives for you in that year and that season of your life.

Be Romantic And Have Sex

Keep doing the things you loved to do when you were

courting or dating. Go on a date at least once a month if not once every two weeks. Did you say you can't afford it? Or you're are too busy? Honey it's much cheaper than a divorce and less time consuming too.

Send love notes to one another throughout the day. If your excuse for not doing this is that you are usually busy at work, let's talk about the useless forwarded whatsapp or Facebook messenger messages you were able to send to people who don't even care about you.

Maintain an active life of intimacy and make sure that it is genuinely pleasurable to the both of you.

Watch Your Mouth

Guard your home. Don't tell people who have no interest in seeing your marriage succeed your intimate personal affairs. If you tell one person, it is no longer between you and your spouse.

Don't nag your spouse and learn to forgive quickly. Understand your differences, accept them and work through them make them your strengths. If you want to change your partner by fire by force, it will not work. Prayer, love and patience are the keys.

Be Careful Where You Get Counsel

For those of you who run to "prophets" often to tell you about your life and family history. Please do not allow a prophet to break up your home in the name of God. Use discernment and wisdom. Be wary of any prophet that tells you to leave your spouse or that your spouse or in-laws are the source of your misfortune or hardship.

How on earth can a person hold a bible in one hand and tell a child of God that is praying for children, that the only way she can get pregnant is to leave her husband and sleep with another man? And why are people buying this type of counsel? Run for your life and your marriage.

Hardships come to every home in different forms they are overcome by prayer not false accusations from a prophet or terminating your marriage and becoming the perpetual source of income for a rogue. The bible says of them in Matthew 7:15 *[You Will Know Them by Their Fruits]* *"Beware of false prophets, who come to you in sheep's clothing, but inwardly they are ravenous wolves."* Their end is destruction because their belly is their God. Don't become one of their victims. If any "prophet" or "Pastor" has spoken evil over your home or life take it to Jesus and cancel their utterances.

Choose What Type Of Marriage You Will Have

Make up your minds together that you will both enjoy your marriage and not endure it and don't settle for anything less. This won't just "happen". It comes in your daily decisions. Building takes work and effort, sweat and tears. It takes a determination to make it in the face of all odds.

Have Fun!

Finally, I've said this before but choose to have fun - my husband and I have a lot of fun, laughing together and our children benefit and do this too in their marriages. Be willing to laugh! We laugh about things that would probably cause other people to fight and argue. We laugh about my weight, his stomach, the way he spoke to me the other day, a huge mistake I made today. Whatever it is, we have determined not to be offended at one another and are willing to laugh at ourselves.

Fill your home with humor!

"Love suffers long and is kind; love does not envy; love does not parade itself, is not puffed up; does not behave rudely, does not seek its own, is not provoked, thinks no evil; does not rejoice in iniquity, but rejoices in the truth; bears all things, believes all things, hopes all things, endures all things."
1 Corinthians 13:4-7

"Through wisdom a house is built, and by understanding it is established; By knowledge the rooms are filled. With all precious and pleasant riches."
Proverbs 24:3

Wishing you a happy, lasting marriage from my home to yours!

Endnotes

Chapter Six
1.   Stock, Pamela. "Marriage After Baby: Problems and Solutions." Parents, Parents, 15 June 2017, www.parents.com/parenting/relationships/staying-close/marriage-after-baby/.

Chapter Ten
1. Donnelly, Denise A. "Sexually Inactive Marriages." Journal of Sex Research, vol. 30, no. 2, 12 Apr. 1993, pp. 171–179., doi:10.1080/00224499309551698.

Chapter Fourteen
1.   Navarra, Dr. Bob. "Addiction Recovery for Couples: Path for Healing or A Ticking Time Bomb?" Couples in Addiction Recovery, 23 Dec. 2013, bobnavarra.wordpress.com/2013/12/23/addiction-recovery-for-couples-path-for-healing-or-a-ticking-time-bomb/.
2.   "Journal of Studies on Alcohol and Drugs" University of Michigan, http://www.jsad.com/toc/jsad/75/3.

Chapter Fifteen
1. Buss, D. M., & Shackelford, T. K. (1997). Susceptibility to infidelity in the first year of marriage. Journal of Research in Personality, 31, 193-221.
2. Savage, Jill. "Rebuilding Trust After an Affair » Higher Appeal." Higher Appeal, 27 July 2016, higherappeal.com/rebuilding-trust-affair/.

Chapter Seventeen
1. Johnson, Michael P. Typology of Domestic Violence Intimate Terrorism, Violent Resistance, and Situational Couple Violence. Hanover, Northeastern University Press, 2010.
2. "Warning Signs of Domestic Violence." National Domestic Violence Hotline, 2014, www.ndvh.org/educate/what_is_dv.html.

Chapter Nineteen
1. "Divorce Facts and Statistics | What Affects Divorce Rates?" Wilkinson & Finkbeiner, LLP, 2015, www.wf-lawyers.com/divorce-statistics-and-facts/.

About The Author

Eyitayo Dada is a marriage counsellor and an internationally known speaker on relationships, dating and marriage. Her joy, warmth and no-nonsense speaking style as well as age-old wisdom has won her the title, "Maama" to thousands across the globe.

Also a practicing Lawyer and an administrator in the Social Services sector for over 25 years, she has helped countless individuals and families enhance their individual and collective well being. With a Ph.D in Pastoral Counseling (HON) from the Canadian Institute Of Christian Counsellors, Eyitayo was named one of the "100 Black Women To Watch in Canada" in 2016.

She has been happily married for over 30 years to Amos Dada. She and her husband live in Toronto, Canada. They are the parents of 5 beautiful daughters, 2 son-in-laws and 2 grandchildren.

To book Maama for speaking engagements
or order more copies of
"Making Your Marriage Work:
Maama's Practical Wisdom for a Lasting Happy
Marriage", visit
www.makingyourmarriagework.ca
or email
tayo@makingyourmarriagework.ca

Facebook/Instagram/Twitter: @EyitayoDada